RECIPES FROM THE WORLD OF TOLKIEN

Thunder Bay Press
An imprint of Printers Row Publishing Group
9717 Pacific Heights Blvd, San Diego, CA 92121
www.thunderbaybooks.com • mail@thunderbaybooks.com

Printers Row Publishing Group is a division of Readerlink Distribution Services, LLC.
Thunder Bay Press is a registered trademark of Readerlink Distribution Services, LLC.

All notations of errors or omissions should be addressed to Thunder Bay Press,
Editorial Department, at the above address. Author, illustration, and rights inquiries
should be addressed to Octopus Publishing Group Ltd Carmelite House, 50 Victoria
Embankment, London EC4Y 0DZ
www.octopusbooks.co.uk

THUNDER BAY PRESS
Publisher: Peter Norton • Associate Publisher: Ana Parker
Acquisitions Editor: Kathryn Chipinka Dalby
Editor: JoAnn Padgett

Produced by Octopus Publishing Group
Publisher: Lucy Pessell
Editor: Sarah Kennedy • Designer: Hannah Coughlin
Editorial Assistant: Emily Martin
Recipe Development: Jane Birch
Contributing Editor: Robert Tuesley Anderson
Senior Production Manager: Peter Hunt

Library of Congress Control Number:
2020934183
ISBN: 978-1-64517-442-4

Printed in China
28 27 26 25 24   8 9 10 11 12

RECIPES FROM THE WORLD OF TOLKIEN

INSPIRED BY THE LEGENDS

Robert Tuesley Anderson

THUNDER BAY
P·R·E·S·S

San Diego, California

CONTENTS

INTRODUCTION

In both *The Hobbit* and *The Lord of the Rings*, warriors and heroes, big and small, Men, Dwarves, Wizards, and Hobbits—Hobbits *especially*—are shown to be interested, even preoccupied, with food and drink. There are dozens of references to breakfasts, second breakfasts, lunches, dinners, and feasts—and plenty more to other foodstuffs, from travelers' waybreads to near-miraculous draughts.

Tolkien's concern with food, however, goes far beyond the merely utilitarian. His descriptions of the aforementioned meals are often detailed and loving—suggesting the real pleasure that the characters and their creator take in eating and drinking. Who can forget Sam's comforting rabbit stew, rustled up in the wilderness to sustain his beloved friend and master Frodo? Or the honeyed cakes and mead of Beorn the skin-changer, or the vegetarian feast created by Tom Bombadil and Goldberry? Tolkien's tour de force in this respect is, of course, the unexpected party that opens *The Hobbit*, where delicious cakes, pies, and other treats accumulate in a mouthwatering pile.

There is a deeper aspect to the omnipresence of food in Tolkien's stories, however. At one level, it contributes to their narrative structure: *The Hobbit* and *The Lord of the Rings* both begin with homely feasts before the adventure properly begins. This pattern repeats itself through the books, with a crisis of suspense and jeopardy followed by a respite often marked by a good meal of some kind, and so on, so that the reader constantly moves between breathless excitement and feelings of cosseted charm. At another level still, the food in the stories sometimes has a real emotional punch. Sam's making of the rabbit stew is an act of love for Frodo, offering a hopeful vision of home amid the despair.

Rivendell

Food in Tolkien is about these things: companionship and friendship, love and hope, and—perhaps most importantly of all—home. No surprise, then, that the Lembas bread of the Elves have a spiritual, even godly, quality about them.

In this book, you will find a rich collection of recipes inspired by the food and dishes in *The Hobbit* and *The Lord of the Rings*. Some like Sam's Coney Stew (page 156), and Beorn's Honey Cakes (page 28) are, to some extent, re-creations of actual dishes found in the books; while others pay homage, more fancifully, to the characters, peoples, and places, like the Roasted Stuffed Pepper Flames (page 84), inspired by the flame-clothed Balrogs, or the Grey Havens Garlicky Grilled Mussels (page 96), in honor of the Elven port.

The recipes are arranged according to the Hobbits' six daily meals—Breakfast, Second Breakfast, Elevenses, Luncheon, Afternoon Tea, and Dinner—though inevitably quite a few could just as well have been included in one section as another. There is a final section on drinks, too, which, like food, plays an important role in Tolkien's tales.

With the above in mind, it's time to explore the smells and tastes of Middle-earth. Enjoy experimenting, discovering and, of course, eating all the delicious ingredients found in these recipes, and let whatever you decide to conjure up transport you straight into Tolkien's legendary world.

Holman Greenhand,
a Hobbit gardener

BREAKFAST

Tolkien's Hobbits like to start their days with a hearty breakfast, and find little more disheartening than setting off on a day's trek on an empty stomach. There is wisdom here, of course, though there are plenty of other, healthier options than Bilbo's favorite of eggs and bacon, and tea and hot buttered toast …

OATMEAL

Packed with fiber, nutrients, and complex carbs, a steaming bowl of oatmeal is the perfect way to provide your body with fuel for the day ahead. To add extra nutrition and flavor, there's a list of Middle-earth inspired toppings for you to choose from, too.

Unlike improvised gruel made from oats and water—the kind of breakfast a weary traveler might make while undertaking a long journey, such as the Hobbits did—oatmeal made at home with full access to milk, honey, fruits, jellies, and nuts can be a sumptuous feast—fit for Hobbits, Dwarves, and Men alike.

SERVES FOUR TO SIX

PREP AND COOK 15 MINUTES

INGREDIENTS

1 ¾ pints dairy or dairy-free milk
2 cups, plus 2 tablespoons water
1 teaspoon vanilla extract
Pinch of ground cinnamon
Pinch of salt
2 cups rolled oats

TOPPING OPTIONS

Beorning-style: Top with a spoon of honey, a scattering of nuts, and a handful of berries.

Hobbit-style: Finish with a spoonful of "Dumbledor" Blueberry and Honey Jelly (page 117) or Spiced Plum Jelly (page 120) and a dollop of cream.

Dwarven-style: Scatter over chopped dried fruit and nuts.

Rohan-style: Stew 2 peeled, cored, and chopped apples with a little brown sugar and water, and spoon over the top.

Númenórean-style: Add a drizzle of maple syrup and a roughly chopped fig, plus a pinch of ground cinnamon.

Gondorian-style: Pit, slice, and lightly grill a peach, and add to the oatmeal with a dash of cream.

1 Put the milk, water, vanilla extract, cinnamon, and salt in a large saucepan over medium heat and bring slowly to a boil. Stir in the oats, then reduce the heat and simmer gently, stirring occasionally, for 8 to 10 minutes until creamy and tender.

2 Spoon the oatmeal into bowls and serve with the topping of your choice.

TRAVELER'S OVERNIGHT OATS

Make this easy-to-prep and easy-to-transport breakfast vegan by using dairy-free milk and yogurt—oat and coconut both work well. You can experiment with flavorings to suit your taste; try adding seeds and nuts, chopped apples or pears, or dried fruit.

When traveling long distances, oats and other grains are a practical food to carry with you. They last a long time if kept dry, and can quickly and easily be made into simple yet filling food. On their long journeys, Tolkien's heroes are likely to have been equipped with some quantity of grains, especially to feed their horses and ponies.

SERVES ONE

PREP AND **COOK** 15 MINUTES, PLUS
OVERNIGHT SOAKING

INGREDIENTS

⅔ cup rolled oats
⅓ to ½ milk
1 tablespoon plain yogurt, plus extra to
  serve (optional)
Drizzle of honey or maple syrup
Fresh fruit of choice, to serve (optional)

For the optional flavorings
¼ teaspoon ground cinnamon and a
  small handful of blueberries
Small handful of raspberries and
  chocolate chips
½ tablespoon cocoa powder and a few
  cherries
½ tablespoon dry unsweetened coconut
  and a few strawberries

1   Combine all the ingredients for the base
of the overnight oats in a container or
glass jar and stir. Add one of the optional
flavorings, stir to combine, and leave in
the fridge overnight.

2   Add extra fruit or yogurt to serve, if desired.

SMOKY STEWED BEANS

You can eat these comforting and filling stewed beans for breakfast the British way—atop hot buttered toast—or for lunch on a baked potato with a little grated cheese sprinkled over. They freeze well so why not make a big batch?

Foods in Middle-earth tend to be simple, filling, and delicious. While beans on toast is not very popular in America, it's one of those quintessential British standby meals that have helped define British food culture. Tolkien's mission in creating Middle-earth was to invent an English mythology, and in doing so he wove timeless elements of English and British culture into his work, including its food (the Fish and Chips on page 142 is another example).

SERVES FOUR
PREP AND COOK 45 MINUTES

INGREDIENTS

2 tablespoons canola oil
1 red onion, cut into wedges
14-ounce can chopped tomatoes
2 tablespoons tomato paste
2 tablespoons dark brown sugar
3 tablespoons red wine vinegar
1 teaspoon smoked paprika
1 teaspoon mustard powder
1 cup, plus 2 tablespoons vegetable stock
2 14-ounce cans cannellini beans, drained and rinsed
Salt and black pepper
2 tablespoons chopped Italian parsley, to garnish

1   Heat the oil in a saucepan, add the onion and fry for
    3 minutes until just starting to soften. Add the tomatoes,
    tomato paste, sugar, vinegar, paprika, mustard powder, and
    stock. Bring to a boil, stirring, then reduce the heat and
    simmer, uncovered, for 20 minutes until reduced slightly.

2   Add the drained beans to the tomato sauce. Simmer for
    an additional 15 to 20 minutes, covered, until thick, then
    season with salt and pepper, and serve on toast, or as
    a baked potato topping with the chopped parsley.

BACON AND MUSHROOM FRITTATA

The smell and sound of sizzling bacon are enough to make any morning feel special. This dish makes a little bacon go a long way and, if there's any frittata left over, you can enjoy it cold for lunch with a side salad.

In The Hobbit, *Bilbo's love of bacon is unparalleled. After sneakily handing over the Arkenstone to Bard the Bowman and the Elvenking to prevent conflict between the Men of Dale, the Elves, and the Dwarves, he returns to the sentry post at the Gate of the Lonely Mountain, promptly falls asleep, and dreams of eggs and bacon. It seems, then, that even after the thrills of burgling treasure and meeting a Dragon, Bilbo still prizes the simple things.*

SERVES FOUR
PREP AND COOK 45 MINUTES

INGREDIENTS

8 cremini mushrooms or mushrooms of
   your choice, about 1 pound in total
1 garlic clove, finely chopped (optional)
Olive oil, for drizzling
4 strips of smoked bacon or sliced ham
6 large eggs
1 tablespoon chopped chives, plus extra
   to garnish
1 tablespoon whole grain mustard
1 tablespoon butter
Salt and black pepper

1   Put the mushrooms on a baking sheet and scatter the garlic over them, if using. Drizzle over a little olive oil, season with salt and pepper and place in a preheated oven, 350°F, for 18 to 20 minutes or until softened. Leave until cool enough to handle.

2   Meanwhile, lay the bacon strips on a foil-lined grill pan and cook under a preheated medium-hot broiler for 5 to 6 minutes, turning once or until slightly crispy. Cool slightly, then slice thickly.

3   Put the eggs, chives, and mustard in a bowl, beat together lightly and season with pepper.

4   Heat a large nonstick skillet with an ovenproof handle, add the butter and melt until it begins to foam.

5   Pour in the egg mixture and cook for 1 to 2 minutes, then add the bacon and cooked mushrooms. Cook for an additional 2 to 3 minutes or until almost set.

6   Place the pan under a preheated hot broiler and cook the frittata for 2 to 3 minutes until set, then cool slightly, sprinkle on some chopped chives and cut into slices to serve.

POTATO AND CABBAGE FRITTER

Known as bubble and squeak in Britain—because the cabbage makes bubbling and squeaking sounds while it cooks—this hearty dish makes the most of leftovers. You can add any cooked veggies you have hanging around in the refrigerator, including peas, carrots, and leeks.

Hamfast "The Gaffer" Gamgee is Samwise Gamgee's father and Bilbo's gardener until Sam takes over the role. Just as young Samwise did, who wouldn't love to spend time at Bag End listening to Bilbo's incredible stories? Stories that spurred Sam's father to exclaim that Elves and Dragons are not for the likes of Hobbits, who are better off keeping to cabbages and potatoes!

SERVES FOUR
PREP AND COOK 15 MINUTES

INGREDIENTS

1 tablespoon butter
4 strips bacon, chopped
1 onion, finely diced
1 garlic clove, minced
1 ¾ cups cooked cabbage, shredded
2 ¼ cups cold mashed potatoes

1 Melt the butter in a pan and add the chopped bacon. As it begins to brown, add the onion and garlic.

2 Add the cabbage and cook for 5 to 6 minutes until it browns slightly. Add the mashed potatoes and mix everything together, pushing the mixture down so that it covers the base of the pan.

3 Cook until the underside is golden brown and sticking to the pan a little, then flip it over like a pancake, and cook the other side until golden brown.

4 Remove from pan and slice to serve.

TRAVELER'S ALL-IN-ONE BREAKFAST IN A PAN

This recipe is perfect accompanied by a pot of hot coffee. Cook this fuss-free vegetarian breakfast in one roasting pan and place in the middle of the table for everyone to help themselves.

SERVES FOUR
PREP AND COOK 45 MINUTES

INGREDIENTS

2 ½ cups cooked potatoes, cubed
4 tablespoons olive oil
Few thyme sprigs
12 button mushrooms, trimmed
12 cherry tomatoes
4 eggs
Salt and black pepper
2 tablespoons chopped parsley, to garnish

1   Spread the potato cubes out in an even layer in a large roasting pan. Drizzle over the oil, scatter over the thyme sprigs, and season with salt and pepper.

2   Bake in a preheated oven, 425°F, for 10 minutes. Stir the potato cubes well, then add the mushrooms and return the roasting pan to the oven for an additional 10 minutes. Add the tomatoes and return the pan to the oven for an additional 10 minutes. Make 4 hollows in between the vegetables and carefully break an egg into each one. Return the pan to the oven for a final 3 to 4 minutes until the eggs are set.

3   Scatter the parsley over the top and serve straight from the pan.

Tolkien's stories are full of long journeys and meals eaten on the road (see page 72). This breakfast recipe is inspired by camping and cooking over an open fire. Made with only one pan but packed with hearty and filling ingredients to fuel a day of trekking, this breakfast will satisfy all manner of travelers for the road ahead.

Following Page:
The Quest of Erebor

BEREN'S POTATO BREAD

This unusual bread is perfect for mopping up the juices from thyme-flecked tomatoes here, but is also wonderful spread with Spiced Apple Butter (page 46), or lightly toasted and buttered to accompany The Soup of Story on page 88.

Among Men, Beren is perhaps the great hero of The Silmarillion. *He steals a Silmaril jewel from Morgoth's crown, defeats the great wolf Carcharoth, and is the only man to return from the dead. Interestingly, he is also one of the few confirmed vegetarian characters in Tolkien's work. He gives up eating meat out of kinship with the animals who help him survive while he lives as a solitary outlaw.*

SERVES FOUR
PREP AND COOK 4 HOURS

INGREDIENTS

1 ¾ cups potatoes, peeled and cut into chunks
1 teaspoon instant fast-acting dry yeast
1 teaspoon superfine sugar
1 tablespoon sunflower oil, plus extra for oiling
Scant 1 ½ cups white bread flour, plus extra for dusting
¾ cup whole-wheat bread flour
2 tablespoons chopped rosemary
1 tablespoon thyme leaves
Salt and black pepper

For the topping
2 tablespoons olive oil
¾ cups mixed-color baby tomatoes, halved
½ teaspoon thyme leaves
½ teaspoon sea salt flakes
Pepper

1 Cook the potatoes in a large saucepan of lightly salted boiling water for 15 to 20 minutes until tender but not flaky. Drain really well, reserving the cooking liquid.

2 Put 6 tablespoons of the cooking liquid into a large bowl and leave to cool until lukewarm. Sprinkle the yeast over the water, then stir in the sugar and set aside for 10 minutes.

3 Mash the potatoes with the oil, then stir in the yeast mixture, and mix well with a wooden spoon. Mix in the flours, herbs, and salt and pepper, then turn out on to a lightly floured surface, and knead well to incorporate the last of the flour. Knead the dough until soft and pliable, then put in a lightly oiled bowl, cover with plastic wrap, and leave to rise in a warm place for 1 hour until well risen.

4 Knead the dough on a lightly floured surface, then roughly shape into a round, place on a baking sheet and lightly cover with oiled plastic wrap. Leave to rise in a warm place for 30 minutes. Score a cross into the dough with a knife and bake in a preheated oven, 425°F, for 35 to 40 minutes until well risen and crusty on top.

5 Transfer to a wire rack to cool for 30 minutes. Cut 4 slices of the bread and lightly toast.

6 Meanwhile, heat the oil for the topping in a skillet, add the tomatoes and cook over high heat for 2 to 3 minutes until softened. Stir in the thyme and salt flakes. Season with pepper and serve with the toasted potato bread.

SPICED PEAR AND CRANBERRY MUFFINS

These cranberry-studded muffins are a great grab-and-go breakfast. The secret to airy, light muffins is not overmixing. Resist the temptation to stir your muffin batter vigorously until smooth—the batter should be only gently stirred and lumps are fine, they'll disperse in the baking.

MAKES TWELVE
PREP AND COOK 35 MINUTES

INGREDIENTS

Scant ½ cup dried cranberries
2 tablespoons boiling water
3 small ripe pears
2 ¼ cups all-purpose flour
3 teaspoons baking powder
1 teaspoon ground cinnamon
½ teaspoon grated nutmeg
⅔ cup superfine sugar, plus extra
   for sprinkling
4 tablespoons (¼ cup) butter, melted
3 tablespoons olive oil
3 eggs
½ cup plain yogurt

1 Put the cranberries in a cup, add the boiling water and leave to soak for 10 minutes. Meanwhile, quarter, core, peel, and dice the pears.

2 Place the flour, baking powder, spices, and sugar in a mixing bowl. Stir the melted butter, oil, eggs, and yogurt together in another bowl, then combine with the flour mixture.

3 Drain the cranberries, add to the flour mixture with the pears and mix briefly, then spoon into paper muffin cases arranged in a 12-hole deep muffin pan and sprinkle with a little extra superfine sugar.

4 Bake in a preheated oven, 400°F, for 15 to 18 minutes until well risen and golden.

5 Leave to cool in the pan for 5 minutes, then transfer to a wire rack. Serve warm or cold. They are best eaten on the day they are made.

The history of Middle-earth is full of gems and jewels, from the Silmarils to the Arkenstone. One place that is brimming with gems is the Glittering Caves—or Aglarond in Sindarin— that lie behind Helm's Deep in the White Mountains. With their high, domed ceilings, sandy floors, and polished walls set with gems, crystals, and veins of ore, it's no wonder that Gimli the Dwarf is astounded by the caves' beauty, so much so that he returns there after the War of the Ring to found a new Dwarven kingdom.

These muffins have bright red cranberries scattered throughout, like gems in a mine. Their warm golden color further echoes the sandy stone of Aglarond.

BEORN'S HONEY CAKES

An excellent breakfast or teatime treat, these little honeyed cakes are a good way to use up over-ripe bananas.

In The Hobbit, *Bilbo's party encounters Beorn the "skin-changer," who as well as being a chieftain of the Beornings is also, it seems, an excellent cook. Beorn's name refers not only to his second form as a bear (the Scandinavian name Björn means exactly that) but also puns on his passion for keeping bees (bears love honey!). Honey cakes are a specialty of his, which he gives to Thorin and Company when he hosts them during the Quest of Erebor. He also has a twice-baked, or cookie-like, version (page 116).*

MAKES TWELVE
PREP AND COOK 45 MINUTES

INGREDIENTS

Scant 1 cup all-purpose flour
1 teaspoon baking powder
¼ teaspoon, baking soda
½ cup, plus 2 tablespoons unsalted
  butter, melted
Generous ⅓ cup light brown sugar
2 eggs, beaten
2 small, very ripe bananas, mashed
4 tablepoons honey

1   Line a 12-cup muffin pan with paper cases.

2   Sift the flour, baking powder, and baking soda
    into a bowl.

3   Mix together the melted butter, sugar, eggs,
    and mashed bananas in a separate bowl.
    Tip in the dry ingredients and mix together
    gently until evenly combined. Divide the cake
    mixture between the paper cases.

4   Bake in preheated oven, 325°F, for 20 to
    25 minutes or until risen and just firm
    to the touch.

5   Transfer to a wire rack and drizzle each
    cake with 1 teaspoon of honey. Serve
    warm or cold.

Beornings

HOBBITS AND FOOD

Hobbits like their food—indeed, their concern with having a full stomach is almost as characteristic of their race as their short stature and hairy feet. Not only are they good at eating, they are good at cooking too, an art they learn even before they learn to read and write (if they manage to do that!). Sam appears to be the best Hobbit cook we meet, able to rustle up a feast out of the most rudimentary ingredients (see the famous Coney Stew on page 156). Though Bilbo also seems to be a more than competent baker.

Tolkien famously drew attention to the close association between Hobbits and food in his Prologue to *The Lord of the Rings*, where he informs us of their love for both laughter and food and their partiality for six meals a day "when they can get them." By the end of the Third Age, the author tells us, plenty is the norm in the Hobbits' homeland, the Shire, and memories of the Days of Dearth (TA 1158–60)—a famine that followed an outbreak of plague—are but a folk memory.

And, if the representatives we meet in Tolkien's tales are anything to go by, the Hobbits do get their regulation six meals: all are a little chubby—some more so than others (Fredegar "Fatty" Bolger is a fine example)—and they spend a lot of their time eating, talking, and thinking food. Tolkien peppers *The Hobbit* itself and *The Lord of the Rings* with references both to his Hobbit heroes' delight in hearty food and, when cast adrift in the wildernesses of Middle-earth, to their worries about where their next meal might come from.

The typical fare of the Hobbits is homely. Bilbo's unexpected tea party gives us the full flavor of the Hobbits' customary diet (as well as an inkling of just how well-stocked a Hobbit's larders—note the plural—could be). To meet his guests' requests, Mr. Baggins successively brings out seed-cakes, buttered scones, raspberry jelly, apple pie, cold chicken, eggs, pickles, salad, and "an extra cake or two," all washed down with ale, porter, wine, and tea and coffee.

This is the food of Tolkien's own childhood in the 1890s and 1900s, and of late Victorian and Edwardian England, at least of the moderately prosperous—solid, unfussy, filling. Even in today's multicultural Britain, Bilbo's tea-cum-dinner party remains a richly nostalgic feast. It also sets the standard against which all other meals in *The Hobbit* and *The Lord of the Rings* will be judged.

SECOND BREAKFAST

Near the beginning of The Hobbit, *Bilbo Baggins—finally rid, so he thinks, of the large party of Dwarves who have been eating him out of house and home since the previous afternoon—is just about to relax by having "a nice little second breakfast" when he is interrupted by Gandalf, calling him away on his adventure … In our world, second breakfast may be little more than a snack, to get us through a mid-morning energy dip, but in its heartiest form—especially at the weekend—it can take the form of "brunch."*

FARMER MAGGOT'S WILD MUSHROOMS ON TOAST

These delicious mushrooms, which are rich in antioxidants as well as being one of the few food sources of essential vitamin D, are perfect as part of a healthy morning meal.

Frodo and his companions' trek through the Shire countryside near the beginning of The Lord of the Rings *provides the reader with a gentle, pastoral vision of Hobbit life—despite the gathering threat of the Black Riders. The iconic moment here is the dinner at Farmer Maggot's house in the Marish, where the Hobbits are served a massive dish of the farmer's famous (and delicious) mushrooms.*

SERVES FOUR
PREP AND COOK 15 MINUTES

INGREDIENTS

2 tablespoons butter
3 tablespoons extra virgin olive oil, plus extra to serve
1 ½ pounds mixed wild mushrooms, such as oyster, shiitake, flat, and button, trimmed and sliced
2 garlic cloves, crushed
1 tablespoon chopped thyme
Grated zest and juice of 1 lemon
2 tablespoons chopped parsley
4 slices of sourdough bread
2 cups mixed salad leaves
Salt and black pepper
Parmesan cheese, to serve

1 Melt the butter with the oil in a skillet. As soon as the butter stops foaming, add the mushrooms, garlic, thyme, lemon zest, and salt and pepper, and cook over medium heat, stirring, for 4 to 5 minutes until tender. Scatter on the parsley and squeeze on a little lemon juice.

2 Meanwhile, toast the bread, then arrange it on serving plates.

3 Top the sourdough toast with an equal quantity of the salad leaves and mushrooms, and drizzle over a little more oil and lemon juice. Scatter with Parmesan shavings and serve immediately.

DRAGON EGGS

The fascinating streaky and mottled appearance of these "dragon eggs" make them a truly exciting morning snack. With their Chinese-inspired flavors, they taste great too!

SERVES FOUR
PREP AND COOK 2 ½ HOURS,
   PLUS COOLING 8 TO 12 HOURS

INGREDIENTS

8 eggs
2 ½ cups water
1 tablespoon light soy sauce
1 tablespoon dark soy sauce
2 tablespoons black tea leaves
2 star anise
1 cinnamon stick
1 tablespoon finely grated rind
   of 1 orange
Salt
Crisp lettuce leaves, to serve

1   Place the eggs in a large saucepan with 1 teaspoon of salt and cover with cold water. Bring to a boil, then reduce the heat, and simmer for 12 minutes. Remove from the heat, drain, and leave to cool. When cool, tap the eggs with the back of a spoon to crack the shells all over, but don't remove the shells.

2   Combine the measured water, soy sauces, ¼ teaspoon of salt, tea leaves, star anise, cinnamon stick, and orange rind in a large saucepan. Bring to the boil, then reduce the heat, cover and simmer for 2 hours. Remove from the heat, add the eggs and leave to stand for at least 8 to 12 hours.

3   Shell the eggs and cut in half, then serve with crisp lettuce leaves for a dragon-inspired brunch dish.

Dragons are the among the most ferocious beasts of Middle-earth. From the wily Glaurung to the mighty Ancalagon the Black, to the golden-red Smaug of the Lonely Mountain, Tolkien's dragons have the ability to wreak unparalleled destruction. Triumph over their dark might by eating them before they hatch.

SPINACH AND SWEET POTATO CAKES

Liven up weekend brunch with these crispy sesame-crusted cakes and serve with soft-poached eggs for dipping them into. For a spicy version, add a little chopped red chili to the potato mixture.

Similar to classic potato hash browns, this variation makes the most of some of the first fresh green vegetables of the spring. Bilbo's gardener, Hamfast Gamgee, "The Gaffer," would have raised a good crop of spinach almost all year round, we imagine.

INGREDIENTS

2 ½ cups sweet potatoes, cut into
    chunks
2 ½ cups spinach leaves
4 to 5 scallions, sliced
1 ½ cups snow peas, finely shredded
½ cup corn
3 tablespoons sesame seeds
¼ cup all-purpose flour
Olive oil, for frying
Salt and black pepper

1   Bring a large saucepan of salted water to a boil, add the sweet potatoes, and cook for about 20 minutes until tender. Drain the potatoes, then return them to the pan, and place over low heat for 1 minute, stirring constantly to evaporate any excess moisture. Lightly mash the potatoes with a fork.

2   Meanwhile, put the spinach leaves in a colander and pour a pan of boiling water over. Rinse the spinach with cold water and squeeze the leaves dry. Stir the wilted spinach into the potatoes, then add the scallions, snow peas, and corn. Season well with salt and pepper and set aside to cool.

3   Use your hands to form the potato mixture into 12 small cakes. Mix the sesame seeds and flour together, and sprinkle the mixture over the cakes.

4   Heat a little oil in a large nonstick skillet until hot but not smoking, and cook 4 of the cakes over moderate heat for 4 to 5 minutes. Once a crisp crust has formed underneath, carefully turn them over, and cook for an additional 4 to 5 minutes on the other side. Keep warm while you repeat until all the cakes are made. You may need to add more oil to the skillet to cook each batch.

POTATO AND SCALLION RÖSTI

Rösti is a delicious way to enjoy potatoes and, here, is given a contemporary twist with a fresh and zingy salsa. For a simpler option, skip the salsa and serve the röstis with grilled tomatoes and mushrooms.

Tolkien famously excised any mention of tomatoes in later, revised editions of The Hobbit, *on the grounds that they were a New World crop. He did not, however, apply the same logic to another American species, the potato. Sam speaks very fondly of "taters," seeming to expect them to be growing wild (along with carrots and turnips) in Ithilien, the once-fair land between Gondor and Mordor. Sam would have loved this dish, then, even if he might have been surprised by the strictly "non-canonical" tomato and avocado salsa!*

SERVES FOUR
PREP AND COOK 45 MINUTES

INGREDIENTS

5 to 6 boiled potatoes (Yukon Gold or
    another all-rounder potato)
6 scallions, finely chopped
2 garlic cloves, very finely chopped
1 large egg, lightly beaten
¼ cup sunflower oil

For the salsa (optional)
2 plum tomatoes, deseeded and roughly
    chopped
1 red chili, deseeded and finely chopped
1 small red onion, halved and very thinly
    sliced
¼ cup finely chopped cilantro
2 avocados, peeled, pitted, and roughly
    sliced
Juice of 2 limes
1 tablespoon avocado oil
Salt and pepper

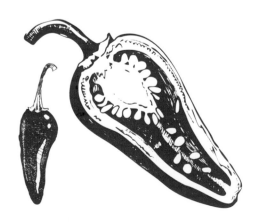

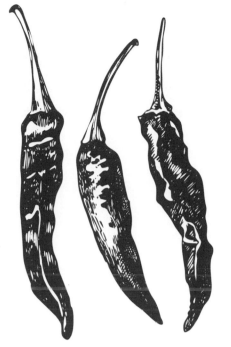

1 Peel and coarsely grate the potatoes. Add the scallions,
   garlic, and egg and use your fingers to combine the
   mixture evenly.

2 Heat a large, nonstick skillet over high heat and add
   half of the oil.

3 Working in batches, divide the potato mixture into
   8 portions. Spoon 4 of the portions into the oil and
   pat down to form röstis about 3 to 4 inches in diameter.
   Cook for 3 to 4 minutes on each side, then carefully
   transfer to a large nonstick baking sheet. Repeat with
   the remaining oil and potato mixture to make 8 röstis.

4 Make the salsa, if desired, by mixing all the ingredients
   together in a bowl. Season well and set aside until ready
   to serve.

5 Serve the röstis accompanied by the salsa.

Following Page:
The Fellowship Arrive at Rivendell

BANNOCK

Bannocks are griddled flatbreads that originated in Scotland. Serve this version, which includes fragrant cumin seeds, with butter and the Gooseberry and Rosemary Jelly on page 48 or, for a sweet version, omit the cumin seeds and add a handful of raisins or currants to the dough instead.

Tolkien's conception of the Elven diet seems to change somewhat over time: we may well get a very different idea of it from reading The Hobbit *than from reading* The Lord of the Rings. *In* The Hobbit, *just before the company reaches the house of Elrond in Rivendell, Bilbo, Gandalf, and the Dwarves come across a party of Elves, who tease this unlikely party of visitors with a mocking song. The Hobbit and the Dwarves must be after some dinner, the Elves sing, as there are faggots roasting and bannocks baking up at the house. Earthy, un-Elvish food indeed, we may think—though a non-Scottish reader may be more puzzled by just what exactly bannocks are!*

MAKES EIGHT
PREP AND COOK 1 HOUR, PLUS
RISING

INGREDIENTS

3 ¼ cups white bread flour,
    plus extra for dusting
⅓ cup cornmeal
1 ½ teaspoons instant fast-acting
    dry yeast
1 teaspoon salt
1 ½ cups warm water
⅓ cup olive oil, plus extra for brushing
1 teaspoon cumin seeds, plus extra to
    serve
Sea salt flakes, to serve (optional)

1   Place the flour, cornmeal, yeast, and salt in
    a bowl and mix together. Add the measured
    water, 3 tablespoons of the oil, and the cumin
    seeds and mix together to form a dough.

2   Knead the dough in an electric mixer for
    5 minutes, or by hand on a lightly floured
    surface for 10 minutes, until the dough is
    soft and springy. Place in a lightly oiled bowl,
    cover with plastic wrap and leave in a warm
    place for about 1 hour until the mixture has
    doubled in size.

3   Tip the dough out on to a lightly floured
    surface, then punch it down and knead
    a couple of times until the air is knocked
    out. Divide the mixture into 8 equal-sized
    balls and keep loosely covered with lightly
    oiled plastic wrap. Roll out each ball until
    ¼ inch thick.

4   Heat a grill pan until smoking hot. Brush over
    the bannocks with a little oil, then cook, in
    batches, for 3 to 5 minutes on each side until
    lightly charred and cooked through. Tear into
    large chunks and serve warm, scattered with
    some cumin seeds and sea salt flakes, if liked.

FOREST FRUIT BRUSCHETTA

These sing of summer, and the sweetness of the berries, contrasted with salty feta and bitter watercress, makes for a refreshing brunch option. If in season, use 4 peaches, halved, pitted, and sliced, instead of strawberries.

One of the iconic scenes in The Lord of the Rings *is the Hobbits' encounter with the mysterious Tom Bombadil and his wife, Goldberry. The couple give the Hobbits a warm, safe place to recuperate after Tom rescues them from the clutches of Old Man Willow in the Old Forest, and for their supper they serve them "bread, butter, cheese with herbs, and ripe berries gathered."*

Here we have reimagined these ingredients together in a beautiful and delicious way: berry bruschetta, an elegant and unexpected variation on the more traditional tomato style.

SERVES SIX
PREP AND COOK 20 MINUTES

INGREDIENTS

2 sourdough baguettes, sliced
2 tablespoons extra virgin olive oil
1 ⅓ cups strawberries, hulled and
   roughly chopped
Large handful of blueberries
¾ cup feta cheese, crumbled
A few watercress sprigs

1 Cut the baguettes into ⅔-inch slices. Place the slices on a baking sheet and drizzle with the oil. Bake in a preheated oven, 400°F, for 10 to 12 minutes until golden.

2 Remove from the oven and top the toasts with the strawberries, blueberries, and the feta cheese and top each with a few watercress sprigs, if desired.

DATE AND SESAME BARS

Easily transportable, these bars are ideal for breakfast on the run or a mid-morning snack. You can change things up by swapping the dates for an equal quantity of other dried fruit—try apricots, cherries, cranberries, or blueberries.

MAKES SIXTEEEN
PREP AND COOK 45 MINUTES

INGREDIENTS

½ cup unsalted butter
Generous ⅓ cup golden superfine sugar*
1 tablespoon honey
½ cup pitted dates, chopped
About 1 cup self-rising flour
Generous ¾ cup steel-cut oatmeal
5 ⅔ tablespoons sesame seeds

* If you cannot find this, you can make it by putting granulated sugar in your food processor. Remeasure after grinding.

1 Grease an 11 x 7-inch shallow baking pan.

2 Put the butter, sugar, and honey in a saucepan and heat gently until the butter has melted, then remove from the heat and stir in the dates.

3 Put the flour and oatmeal in a bowl. Add the sesame seeds, reserving 2 tablespoons, pour in the butter mixture, and mix until combined.

4 Spoon the mixture into the prepared pan and level the surface. Scatter over the reserved sesame seeds.

5 Bake in a preheated oven, 350°F, for 20 to 25 minutes or until golden and just firm to the touch. Leave to cool in the tin, then transfer to a board, and cut into 16 bars.

We might imagine these delicious bars, packed with dates, eaten by the nomadic peoples of the Harad as a pick-me-up as they journey through the desert and debatable lands to the south of Gondor.

SPICED APPLE BUTTER

A truly versatile recipe, this can be enjoyed spread on toast, scones, and muffins, as a condiment with cheese and crackers, dolloped on top of pancakes and waffles, stirred into the Oatmeal on page 12 or added to the Traveler's Overnight Oats on page 14.

This recipe takes its inspiration from the scene in The Lord of the Rings *where, as the Hobbits and their new companion, Strider, leave Bree, Sam chucks an apple at the odious Bill Ferny, who is lurking behind a hedge. A waste of a good apple, indeed—so here is something better to do with this fruit!*

MAKES THREE TO FOUR JARS
PREP AND COOK 2 HOURS

INGREDIENTS

7 ½ cups cooking apples, roughly
   chopped
1 cinnamon stick
1 teaspoon freshly grated nutmeg
1 lemon, chopped
2 cups water
Generous 3 cups granulated sugar

1   Add the apples, spices, chopped lemon, and water to a preserving pan. Bring to a boil, then reduce the heat, and simmer, covered, for 1 hour or until the fruit is reduced to a pulp.

2   Purée in small batches in a food processor.

3   Press the mixture through a fine sieve, then weigh the resulting purée and put it into a clean pan. For every 1 pound of purée add scant 2 cups sugar and cook over low heat, stirring continuously, until the sugar has completely dissolved. Increase the heat to medium, then cook for about 30 minutes, stirring frequently, until the mixture is reduced by half and is thick and glossy, and falls slowly from a wooden spoon.

4   Ladle into warm, dry, sterilized jars, filling to the very top. Cover with screw-top lids, or with waxed discs and cellophane tops secured with elastic bands. Label and leave to cool.

GOOSEBERRY AND ROSEMARY JELLY

The savory hint that gooseberry and rosemary adds to the sweetness of the apple makes for a full-bodied jelly that is excellent on toast for breakfast and works equally well as a condiment to serve with oily fish.

This jelly is inspired by Samwise Gamgee's love of herbs. When cooking his Coney Stew on the journey to Mordor (see the recipe on page 156), Sam asks Gollum/Sméagol to find some herbs to add some flavor (though he ends up foraging for them himself). A skilled gardener, it is likely that the resourceful Hobbit would have had fresh herbs handy in the kitchen garden at Number 3, Bagshot Row, and would doubtless use them at every opportunity.

MAKES THREE TO FOUR JARS

PREP AND COOK 1 HOUR, PLUS STRAINING

INGREDIENTS

9 cups gooseberries*, no need to cut off the tops and bottoms

3 ½ cups water

4 to 5 stems fresh rosemary

4 ⅓ cups granulated sugar

1 tablespoon butter (optional)

* If gooseberries are unavailable, the best substitute would be a tart fruit like fresh cranberries, red currants, or rhubarb.

1   Add the gooseberries, measured water, and rosemary
    to a preserving pan—a low-sided, wide, stainless-steel
    saucepan—so that the jam cooks quickly. Avoid aluminum
    because the acid in the fruit will react with it. Bring to a
    boil, then cover, and simmer gently for 20 to 30 minutes,
    stirring and mashing the fruit from time to time with a
    fork until soft.

2   Leave to cool slightly, then pour into a scalded jelly bag
    suspended over a large bowl, and allow to drip for several
    hours.

3   Measure the clear liquid and pour back into the rinsed
    pan. Weigh 2 ¼ cups sugar for every 16 ounces of liquid,
    then pour into the pan. Heat gently, stirring from time to
    time, until the sugar has dissolved.

4   Bring to a boil, then boil rapidly until setting point is
    reached (10 to 15 minutes). If there is scum on the top
    of the jelly, skim it off with a slotted spoon or stir the
    butter into the jelly to disperse it.

5   Ladle into warm, dry, sterilized jars, filling to the very
    top. Cover with screw-top lids, or with waxed discs and
    cellophane tops secured with elastic bands. Label and leave
    to cool.

ELEVENSES

There is some debate among Tolkien fans about whether elevenses is a different meal from second breakfast and quite how to account for the Hobbits' six meals a day. Elevenses is certainly a common English term for a late-morning snack, but Tolkien makes use of it just once, in his description of the "long-expected party" (it's at elevenses that the day's feasting begins). Moreover, Bilbo eats second breakfast as late as ten-thirty, just half an hour before, so the two meals seem to all but coincide time-wise. All that matters, perhaps, is that Hobbits like their food … and plenty of it.

MUSHROOM PASTRY CAULDRONS

These delicious mouthfuls of pastry with a savory filling are a perfect late-morning treat. You can vary the herbs, depending on what you have on hand, but mushrooms and tarragon go especially well together.

> In some of Tolkien's drafts for what eventually became The Silmarillion, *during the Ages of the Trees, the Valar gather the dewy light of Telperion, the Silver Tree, and collect it in the cauldron Silindrin. Eventually the contents of the cauldron are used in the creation of the sun after the destruction of the Two Trees by Melkor and Ungoliant.*
>
> *These little pastry cauldrons are inspired by this great cauldron from which the sun was born. Delight in their warmth and reflect on the sun's powerful light.*

MAKES SIXTEEN
PREP AND COOK 30 MINUTES

INGREDIENTS

½ cup butter, divided
6 ready-made filo pastry sheets
1 small onion, finely chopped
1 garlic clove, chopped
2 ½ cups mixed mushrooms, trimmed
   and thinly sliced
½ cup mascarpone cheese
2 teaspoons chopped herbs, such as
   tarragon, chervil, and chives, plus
   extra to garnish (optional)
Salt and black pepper

1 Melt half the butter. Brush over 3 sheets of filo pastry and sandwich together. Repeat with another 3 sheets, then cut each into 6 squares. Grease a 12-hole muffin pan, place a filo square into each hole, and gently push down. Bake in a preheated oven, 375°F, for 8 to 10 minutes until crisp.

2 Meanwhile, melt the remaining butter in a skillet and cook the onion and garlic over medium heat for 6 to 7 minutes, stirring occasionally, until softened and golden. Add the mushrooms and fry for an additional 3 to 4 minutes until softened.

3 Stir in the mascarpone and herbs, add a pinch of salt and pepper, then remove from the heat. Spoon the filling into the pastry cases, top with snipped chives and serve warm.

CRAM

Dense and filling, these seeded flatbreads are the perfect vehicle for all kinds of toppings from pickles and cheese to smoked salmon and cured meats. Experiment with your favorite toppings and take these with you on your next picnic. Stored in an airtight tin, they will keep for up to a week.

MAKES TWENTY
PREP AND COOK 40 MINUTES

INGREDIENTS

Generous ¾ cup steel-cut oats
Generous ½ cup all-purpose flour, plus extra for dusting
¼ cup mixed seeds, such as poppy seeds, flax seeds, and sesame seeds
½ teaspoon celery salt or sea salt
½ teaspoon freshly ground black pepper
4 tablespoons unsalted butter, chilled and diced
5 tablespoons cold water

1　Put the oatmeal, flour, seeds, salt, and pepper in a bowl or food processor. Add the butter and rub in with the fingertips or process until the mixture resembles bread crumbs. Add the measured water and mix or blend to a firm dough, adding a little more water if the dough feels dry.

2　Roll out the dough on a lightly floured surface to ⅛ inch thick. Cut out 20 rounds using a 2 ½-inch plain or fluted cookie cutter, re-rolling the trimmings to make more. Place slightly apart on a large, greased baking sheet.

3　Bake in a preheated oven, 350°F, for about 25 minutes until firm. Transfer to a wire rack to cool.

Cram is a type of traveling bread made by the men of Dale both for their own use and to sell to the Dwarves of Erebor.

LEMBAS BREAD

With the hint of spiciness from the chili, this bread is delicious warm from the oven alongside the Smoky Stewed Beans (page 16), or simply accompanied by a few rashers of crispy bacon. It's also very good with mature cheddar cheese and a few Sweet Pickled Cucumbers (page 59) for lunch.

Lembas bread feeds the soul even more than the belly, helping travelers maintain the willpower to overcome tremendous obstacles and intimidating distances. Galadriel gifts the Fellowship a stock of Lembas breads, each wrapped in mallorn leaves to sustain them during the hardships ahead.

According to The Silmarillion, *Lembas is first made by Yavanna, the Valarian queen responsible for all things that grow on the earth, using a special corn that grows in Aman. It is therefore likely that Lembas would have been similar in texture and appearance to a deliciously comforting cornbread.*

MAKES SIXTEEN SQUARES
PREP AND COOK 45 MINUTES

INGREDIENTS

Generous 1 cup all-purpose flour
1 cup cornmeal
1 teaspoon salt
2 teaspoons baking powder
1 tablespoon superfine sugar
3 tablespoons grated Parmesan cheese
Handful of fresh parsley leaves, chopped
1 red chili, deseeded and finely chopped
3 tablespoons olive oil
2 eggs, beaten
½ pint buttermilk

1 Oil an 8-inch square cake pan.

2 Sift together the flour, cornmeal, salt, and baking powder into a large bowl. Stir in the sugar, Parmesan, parsley, and chili.

3 Mix together the oil, eggs, and buttermilk in a separate bowl, then gently stir into the dry ingredients until combined.

4 Pour the mixture into the prepared pan and place in a preheated oven, 375°F, for 30 to 35 minutes until golden.

5 Remove from the oven and transfer to a wire rack to cool slightly, before cutting into 16 squares. This bread can be eaten warm or cold and is best eaten on the day it is made.

Yavanna

ELVISH WHITE BREAD ROLLS

These rolls are ideal as an accompaniment to soups and stews, and would be perfect alongside the Lake-town Beef Pot Roast (page 154). For a cheese and onion variation, replace the seeds with 5 scallions, very finely chopped and lightly cooked for a minute in 1 tablespoon of olive oil. Once glazed, sprinkle with 3 tablespoons of freshly grated Parmesan cheese.

Lembas may be the most famous Elvish bread, but it does not appear to be something that's eaten on a daily basis because, we are told, a single bite can fill a Man's stomach for a whole day. In their normal daily lives, Elves enjoy a delicious light and airy white bread, as discovered by Frodo and his companions when they come across a party of High Elves in the Green-Hill Country of the Shire.

MAKES TWELVE ROLLS
PREP AND COOK 2 HOURS, INCLUDING RESTING TIME

INGREDIENTS

¼ ounce active dry yeast
1 cup warm (not hot) water
About 3 cups white bread flour, plus
   extra for dusting
1 teaspoon salt, plus a pinch
2 tablespoons butter, cut into cubes
4 tablespoons sunflower seeds
2 tablespoons poppy seeds
2 tablespoons pumpkin seeds
1 egg yolk
Salt
1 tablespoon water

1 Sprinkle the yeast over the measured warm water, stir well, and set aside for 10 minutes until it becomes frothy. Sift the flour and salt into a separate large bowl, and add the butter. Rub the butter into the flour until the mixture resembles fine bread crumbs. Add all the seeds and stir.

2 Make a well in the center and add the yeast mixture. Stir well with a wooden spoon, then use your hands to mix to a firm dough.

3 Knead for 5 minutes until the dough feels firm, elastic, and is no longer sticky. Return to the bowl, cover with plastic wrap, and set aside in a warm place for 30 minutes until the dough has doubled in size.

4 Turn out the dough, punch down, and knead again before you divide into 12 pieces. Knead each piece briefly, then form into a roll shape, or roll each piece into a long sausage shape, and form into a loose knot. Place the rolls on a lightly greased baking sheet, cover with a clean dish towel and set aside in a warm place for 30 minutes until almost doubled in size.

5 Mix the egg yolk in a small bowl with a pinch of salt and the measured cold water, and brush over the rolls to glaze. Bake in a preheated oven, 400°F, for 15 to 20 minutes until it is golden and sounds hollow when tapped lightly on the base. Remove from the oven and allow to cool a little.

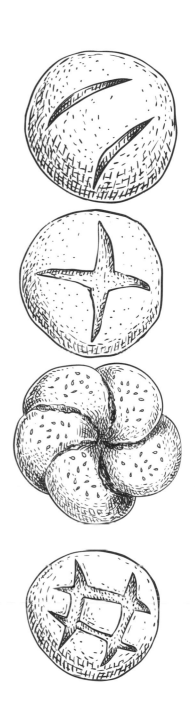

Gandalf

SWEET PICKLED CUCUMBERS

Just the thing to perk up all kinds of sandwiches with their piquant taste, these are also great with beef and hot-smoked trout, and as an addition to a cheese board. Add 2 teaspoons of mustard seeds for a spicier version.

Pickling and preserving were a key skill of the Victorian housewife and cook, but also, it seems, of Hobbits. Bilbo, certainly, must have a good stock of pickles in his larders, as Gandalf seems to know when he asks the beleaguered Hobbit to bring some out along with the cold chicken. Being a Wizard has to have some advantages!

MAKES 3 JARS
PREP AND COOK 30 MINUTES, PLUS SOAKING 4 HOURS AND COOLING 3 TO 4 WEEKS

INGREDIENTS

2 large cucumbers, thinly sliced
1 medium onion, thinly sliced
3 tablespoons plus 1 teaspoon salt
1 ½ cups white wine vinegar
Scant 2 cups granulated sugar
½ teaspoon ground turmeric
2 teaspoons fennel seeds
½ teaspoon dried crushed red chilies
¼ teaspoon peppercorns, roughly crushed

1   Layer the cucumbers, onions, and salt in a bowl, cover with a plate and weight down, then leave to soak for 4 hours.

2   Meanwhile, pour the vinegar into a saucepan, add the sugar and the remaining ingredients, and heat gently, stirring from time to time, until the sugar has dissolved, then leave to cool.

3   Tip the cucumber and onions into a colander and drain off the liquid. Rinse with plenty of cold water and drain well. Reheat the vinegar mixture until just boiling, add the drained cucumber and onion, cook for 1 minute, then lift out of the vinegar with a slotted spoon and pack into warm, dry, sterilized jars. Boil the remaining vinegar mixture for 4 to 5 minutes until syrupy, then leave to cool. Pour the cold vinegar mixture over the cucumber slices to completely cover and to fill the jars to the top (adding a little extra vinegar if needed).

4   Screw on lids, label and leave to mature in a cool, dark place for 3 to 4 weeks.

DWARVEN SPICED PICKLED BEETS

Homemade pickled beets is a classic accompaniment to cold meats and cheese. This spicy, punchy version can be served sliced into salads and sandwiches, or as topping for Cram (page 53).

Living in their underground mines means that Tolkien's Dwarves would probably have needed to rely on preserved foods between deliveries from the surface. This recipe takes a vegetable that can be stored a long while in a cellar and extends its life by an extra 3 to 4 weeks. These pickled beets can be a much-needed flavor injection at the end of a long winter.

MAKES THREE JARS
PREP AND COOK 1 TO 1 ½ HOURS, PLUS COOLING 3 TO 4 WEEKS

INGREDIENTS

10 beets, leaves trimmed to about ¾ inch from the tops
2 cups malt vinegar
⅔ cup granulated sugar
1 ½ inch piece of ginger, peeled and finely chopped
4 teaspoons allspice berries, roughly crushed
½ teaspoon black peppercorns, roughly crushed
½ teaspoon salt

1   Cook the beets in a saucepan of boiling water for 30 minutes to 1 hour, depending on their size, or until a knife can be inserted into the largest one easily. Drain, leave to cool, then peel off the skins with a small knife.

2   Meanwhile, pour the vinegar into a saucepan and add the sugar and remaining ingredients. Heat gently, stirring from time to time, until the sugar has dissolved. Increase the heat and simmer for 3 minutes, then remove from the heat and leave to cool.

3   Cut the beets into chunks and pack into warm, dry, sterilized jars. Pour over the cold vinegar mixture to cover the beets completely and so that the vinegar comes to the top of the jars (adding a little extra vinegar if needed).

4   Screw on lids, label and leave to mature in a cool, dark place for 3 to 4 weeks.

PICKLED PEACHES

Enjoy the flavor of summer in colder months with these quick and easy pickled peaches. Pair with roast pork, chicken, duck or strong cheese.

The real-world peach originates in China and first came to Europe via Persia, the country which gives it its name (from the Latin for "Persian apple") in many European languages. While they are unmentioned by Tolkien in his books, we might well imagine peaches growing in the Mediterranean climate of Gondor, perhaps in the green and well-watered region of Lebennin, which in Middle-earth sits at a similar latitude to the south of Italy, which is also famous for its peaches.

MAKES ONE LARGE JAR
PREP AND COOK 2 HOURS

INGREDIENTS

1 cup white malt vinegar
2 ¼ cups granulated sugar
1 teaspoon whole cloves
1 teaspoon whole allspice berries
3-inch piece cinnamon stick, halved
2 pounds small peaches, halved and stoned

1   In a large saucepan, gently heat the vinegar, sugar, and spices until the sugar has dissolved. Add the peachss and cook very gently for 4 to 5 minutes until just tender but still firm. Using a slotted spoon, pack the peaches tightly into a large warm, dry, and sterilized jar.

2   Boil the pickling syrup for 2 to 3 minutes to concentrate the flavors, then pour over the fruit, filling the jar to the very top. Top up with a little warm vinegar if needed.

3   Add a small piece of crumpled waxed paper to stop the fruit from rising out of the vinegar in the jar. Screw or clip on the lid, label, and leave to cool.

4   After a few hours, the peaches will begin to rise in the jar, but as they become saturated with the syrup they will sink once more; at this point they will be ready to eat. A properly sealed jar should keep for 6 weeks.

PORK PIE

A recipe for all occasions, this pork pie, though it takes a while to make, is great as part of a buffet, goes down well as a late-morning snack, and is perfect for picnics and lunch with sliced tomatoes and pickles—try it with the Sweet Pickled Cucumbers on page 59.

At the beginning of The Hobbit, *Bombur, the fattest of the 13 Dwarves who make up Thorin and Company, puts in an order for pork pie and salad from Bilbo shortly after arriving at Bag End. Both pigs and boars appear occasionally in Tolkien's Middle-earth books—notably the monstrous Boar of Everholt slain by King Folca of Rohan—though it's mostly in the form of bacon that we get to meet them!*

MAKES TWELVE PIES
PREP AND COOK 1 ½ HOURS

INGREDIENTS

1 bunch scallions, finely chopped
Pinch of chili flakes
½ pound pork loin, finely chopped
5 slices bacon, finely chopped
Small bunch chives, chopped
Small bunch parsley, finely chopped
Salt and black pepper
12 quail's eggs*, soft-boiled and peeled
1 egg, beaten

For the pastry
1 ½ cups all-purpose flour
Pinch of salt
½ cup butter, cubed
2 to 3 tablespoons water, to mix

* If quail's eggs are not readily available, substitute 3 slices of hard-boiled egg instead. 4 quail's eggs is the equivalent of 1 chicken egg.

Dwarves

1   First make the pastry. In a large bowl mix the flour with the salt. Using your fingertips, rub the butter into the flour until the mixture resembles bread crumbs.

2   Add the water very gradually while using a knife to mix. Lightly knead the dough to bring it together into a ball, then wrap it in plastic wrap, and chill in the refrigerator for 30 minutes.

3   Meanwhile, make the filling. Mix together the scallions, chili flakes, pork loin, bacon, herbs, and salt and pepper.

4   Lightly grease a 12-cup muffin pan and line each with a strip of waxed paper. This will make the pies easier to take out of the pan.

5   Remove the pastry from the refrigerator. On a lightly floured surface, roll out the chilled pastry and cut 12 x 4-inch rounds for the pie cases and 12 x 3-inch rounds for the lids. Carefully press the larger rounds into the holes of the greased muffin pan.

6   Half fill each case with the filling, top with a soft-boiled quail's egg, then add another layer of filling.

7   Brush the top edge of each pie with a little beaten egg and place a small round of pastry on top, pressing together to seal.

8   Make a small hole in the top of each pie to allow steam to escape, then brush each with more beaten egg to glaze. Bake for 20 minutes in a preheated oven, 400°F, then reduce the temperature to 325°F and cook for an additional 25 to 30 minutes until the pastry is golden.

9   Leave to cool in the pan for 5 minutes before transferring to a wire rack to cool completely.

BEORN'S WARM BAKED CHEESE

What could be nicer than warm, oozy cheese, enhanced with sweet honey, tart cranberries, and crunchy pecans? Ideal as a light meal or a starter, all this needs is plenty of fresh crusty bread for scooping and eating.

Honey—along with plenty of cream and cheese—features heavily in the vegetarian diet of the Beornings, a shape-changing people for whom Tolkien seems to have taken inspiration from the Berserkers, the Viking "bear-shirt" warriors.

To these staples, we have added some dried berries and nuts, which real bears are quite fond of too. This appetizer will satisfy the bear inside every Man, Dwarf, and Hobbit.

SERVES FOUR
PREP AND **COOK** 20 MINUTES

INGREDIENTS

1 whole baby Brie or
   Camembert in a box
3 tablespoons honey
¼ cup pecans
Handful of dried cranberries
Thyme sprigs

1   Remove any packaging from the cheese. Place the cheese on parchment paper on a baking sheet and drizzle generously with honey. Cook in a preheated oven, 400°F, for 15 minutes.

2   Meanwhile, toast the pecans in a small skillet for 3 to 5 minutes until lightly browned, then set aside.

3   Take the cheese from the oven and cut a small cross in the center. Scatter with the pecans, dried cranberries, and thyme and serve with crusty bread.

ALE, APPLE AND MUSTARD CHUTNEY

An excellent and unusual way to use up a glut of cooking apples, this tangy chutney will take your cold beef and ham sandwiches to a new level. It's really easy to make as all it needs is the occasional stir as it bubbles away in the kitchen.

MAKES FOUR JARS
PREP AND COOK 2 ½ HOURS

INGREDIENTS

6 cups cooking apples, quartered, cored, peeled, and diced
4 cups onions, finely chopped
1 cup celery, diced
2 ¾ cups pitted dates, diced
16 ounces brown ale
½ cup malt vinegar
1 ½ cups turbinado sugar
2 tablespoons white mustard seeds, roughly crushed
1 teaspoon ground turmeric
1 teaspoon salt
1 teaspoon peppercorns, roughly crushed

1 Add all the ingredients to a stainless-steel jam pan and cook, uncovered, over gentle heat for 1 ¾ to 2 hours, stirring from time to time, but more frequently toward the end of cooking as the chutney thickens.

2 Ladle into warm, dry, sterilized jars, filling to the very top, and pressing down well. Disperse any air pockets with a skewer or small knife and cover with screw-top lids.

3 Label and leave to mature in a cool, dark place for at least 3 weeks.

Ales and apples both seem quintessentially Hobbitish, so we may well imagine this chutney being enjoyed by Sam's father, Hamfast—known as "The Gaffer"—alongside a chunk of cheese, a hunk of bread, and, of course, a pint or two down at the Green Dragon in Bywater.

CRICKHOLLOW APPLE LOAF

Delicious served spread with butter, this will keep for up to a week in an airtight tin—though it is likely to be eaten long before then! If you are making this for children, use apple juice instead of the cider.

Crickhollow is an out-of-the way location in Buckland across the Brandywine River from the Shire proper. It is Frodo's first destination upon leaving Bag End, on his quest to smuggle the One Ring to Rivendell. To help cover his tracks, he buys a house there with a wide lawn, low trees, and an outer hedge.

Given Hobbits' love of eating and gardening, it's quite likely that at least some of the "low" trees on Frodo's Crickhollow property were apple trees, which stay small throughout their lives. This apple loaf might have been a treat baked in the Crickhollow house kitchen using fruit from the garden.

MAKES ONE LOAF
PREP AND COOK 1 TO 1 ½ HOURS,
PLUS SOAKING 4 HOURS

INGREDIENTS

1 cup dry cider (less sugar) or cloudy
    apple juice
1 large cooking apple, about 1 cup in
    total, cored, peeled and chopped
1 ¼ cups mixed dried fruit
Generous ¾ cup superfine sugar
2 ¼ cups self-rising flour
2 eggs, beaten
1 tablespoon sunflower seeds
1 tablespoon pumpkin seeds

1   Pour the cider into a saucepan, add the apple
    and dried fruit, and bring to a boil. Simmer
    for 3 to 5 minutes until the apple is just
    tender but still firm. Remove the pan from
    the heat and leave to soak for 4 hours.

2   Mix the sugar, flour, and eggs into the soaked
    fruit and stir well.

3   Grease and line the base and 2 long sides of
    a 2-pound loaf pan with oiled waxed paper.
    Spoon the mixture into the prepared pan and
    spread the surface level. Sprinkle with the
    seeds and bake in the center of a preheated
    oven, 325°F, for 1 hour to 1 hour 10 minutes
    until well risen, the top has slightly cracked,
    and a skewer inserted into the center comes
    out clean.

4   Leave to cool in the pan for 10 minutes, then
    loosen the edges and lift out of the pan using
    the lining paper.

5   Transfer to a wire rack, peel off the lining
    paper, and leave to cool completely. Serve cut
    into slices and spread with a little butter.

WESTFARTHING FAIRINGS

These delicate cookies are perfect with a cup of tea and will keep in an airtight tin for up to three days. For a variation, swap the light corn syrup for maple syrup.

The Shire is divided into four regions called Farthings—from the Old English feorthing, *or fourth part. Westfarthing is home to the capital of the Shire, the town of Michel Delving, and Hobbiton, where Bilbo and Frodo's home, Bag End, is located. We think these little cookies pair perfectly with a cup of tea and are perfect for serving to guests who visit in between those six Hobbit meals.*

MAKES TWELVE COOKIES
PREP AND COOK 35 MINUTES

INGREDIENTS

About ¾ cup all-purpose flour
1 teaspoon baking powder
½ teaspoon baking soda
½ teaspoon ground cinnamon
½ teaspoon ground ginger
¼ teaspoon ground allspice or mixed spice
Finely grated zest of 1 lemon
4 tablespoons butter, diced
¼ cup superfine sugar
2 tablespoons light corn syrup

1 Mix the flour, baking powder, baking soda, spices, and lemon zest together in a mixing bowl. Rub in the butter with your fingertips until the mixture resembles fine breadcrumbs.

2 Stir in the sugar, add the syrup, and mix together with a spoon. Squeeze the crumbs together with your hands to form a ball.

3 Shape the dough into a log, then slice into 12 pieces. Roll each piece into a ball and arrange 2 inches apart on greased cookie sheets, leaving space between for them to spread during cooking.

4 Cook one sheet at a time in the center of a preheated oven, 350°F, for 8 to 10 minutes or until cracked and golden.

5 Leave to harden for 1 to 2 minutes, then loosen and transfer to a wire rack to cool completely.

CHERRY AND ALMOND TRAYBAKE

Use fresh cherries when they are in season, instead of candied, but you will need to eat the cake up quickly—it will be more moist so won't keep for more than a day or two. A traybake is a caken baked in a shallow square or rectangular pan and served from it.

The Ents—shepherds of the trees—are among the most mysterious creatures in Tolkien's works—yet more mysterious still are the Entwives. Tolkien tells us their sad story through the mouth of the Ent leader Treebeard: how, long ago, they left their male spouses to tend to the "lesser trees"—the trees of orchards and gardens—and to teach Men the arts of agriculture and horticulture. This moreish (causing one to want to have more) traybake is inspired by the memory of the lost and much-missed Entwives, and by their well-tended cherry trees.

MAKES TEN SQUARES
PREP AND COOK I HOUR

INGREDIENTS

Scant I ¾ cups self-rising flour
I teaspoon baking powder
7 tablespoons unsalted butter, chilled and diced
½ cup, plus I tablespoon white caster/ superfine sugar
I egg, beaten
½ cup milk
I teaspoon almond extract
I ½ cups natural candied cherries (aka glacé cherries), halved, or I ¾ fresh, pitted
⅔ cup slivered almonds
Sifted confectioners' sugar, for dusting

1 Grease and line a 9 inch square shallow baking pan.

2 Combine the flour, baking powder, and butter in a bowl or food processor until the mixture resembles bread crumbs. Add the superfine sugar and combine.

3 Mix the egg, milk, and almond extract. Add to the dry mixture with half the cherries and stir until evenly combined.

4 Spoon the mixture into the prepared pan and spread in an even layer. Scatter over the remaining cherries, then the flaked almonds.

5 Bake in a preheated oven, 350°F, for 25 to 30 minutes or until golden and just firm to the touch. Leave to cool in the pan, then transfer to a board and peel off the lining paper. Dust with sifted confectioners' sugar and cut into squares.

BARLIMAN BUTTERBUR'S BLACKBERRY PIE

Make the most of late-summer bounty with this tart, or pie, which can be served warm or cold as a mid-morning treat or, with whipped cream, as a dessert. The lattice pastry topping looks very impressive but is easy to do.

For almost all the Hobbits of the Shire, the Prancing Pony inn in the village of Bree, out on the Great East Road where it meets the Greenway, represents the limit of their geographic knowledge. It seems that only the most intrepid of Tolkien's Bucklanders occasionally venture through the Hay Gate and make a visit to the inn. Perhaps one of their incentives might have been the promise of blackberry pie, a speciality on the menu of the Pony's forgetful innkeeper, Barliman Butterbur.

SERVES EIGHT

PREP AND COOK I HOUR, PLUS CHILLING AND COOLING

INGREDIENTS

3 ¼ cups blackberries
Juice of ½ lemon
½ cup, plus I tablespoon superfine sugar
2 tablespoons cornstarch, mixed with a
  little water to form a paste

For the pastry
I⅓ cups all-purpose flour, plus extra
  for dusting
7 tablespoons butter, diced
About ¼ cup confectioners' sugar, plus
  extra for dusting
About ½ cup ground almonds
Grated zest of I lemon
2 egg yolks

1   Make the pastry. Add the flour and butter to a bowl and rub in with your fingertips or an electric mixer until you have fine crumbs. Stir in the confectioners' sugar, almonds, and lemon zest, then the egg yolks, and mix to form a dough. Chill for 15 minutes.

2   Knead the pastry, then cut off and reserve a quarter. Roll out the remainder thinly on a lightly floured surface to fit a buttered 9 ½-inch fluted, loose-bottomed tart pan. Press the pastry over the base and sides of the pan.

3   Trim off the excess and add the trimmings to the reserved pastry. Chill the tart and trimmings for 15 minutes.

4   Add half the blackberries, the lemon juice, and superfine sugar to a saucepan and simmer for 5 minutes until the blackberries are soft. Stir in the cornstarch paste and cook over high heat, stirring until the fruit compote thickens. Leave to cool.

5   Spread the blackberry compote over the tart base, then sprinkle the remaining blackberries over the top. Brush the pastry edge with water. Roll out the trimmings and cut into ½ inch wide strips, and arrange as a lattice over the pie, pressing the edges but not trimming off the excess.

6   Bake the pie on a baking sheet in a preheated oven, 375°F, for 25 to 30 minutes until the pastry is golden and the base is cooked. Trim off the excess pastry from the lattice. Transfer to a serving plate, dust with confectioners' sugar, and serve.

FOOD ON THE GO

In the preindustrial world of Middle-earth, travel—sometimes undertaken by horse, occasionally by horse and cart, but most often on foot—is painfully slow. Only the Eagles and a quasi-magical horse like Shadowfax are able to cover vast distances quickly. For this reason, while there seems to be the occasional inn offering homecooked fare, for the most part travelers must fend for themselves, carrying vital supplies with them and cooking, where safe and possible, over an open campfire. They also have to carry some basic cooking equipment. Sam's pack, we learn in *The Lord of the Rings*, contains a few precious items: a tinderbox, two shallow pans, a wooden spoon, a two-pronged fork, skewers and "a dwindling treasure" of salt.

Fortunately, there seems to a number of foods specifically made for the long-distance traveler or warrior on the march. The Elves make Lembas, or Waybread (page 54), which, according to legend, is a kind of cornbread originally made by the Vala Yavanna for the Elves undertaking the Great Journey to Aman. Wrapped in mallorn leaves and left unbroken, we are told that Lembas can stay fresh and sweet for "many many days," and just one of the breads will keep a traveler on his feet for a whole day, even if he is one of the tall Men of Minas Tirith.

Men have their own kind of Waybread, too, even if of a rather less miraculous kind. The Men of Lake-town produce a nourishing, if uninspiring, hard biscuit known as Cram (we have devised a much more delicious version;

page 53), while the Beorning chieftain Beorn makes, to own secret recipe, twice-baked honey cakes (page 116), which, he claims, can help sustain travelers during a long march.

All these are well and good, but nothing can beat a proper, cooked meal, which, even on the most arduous trek, can conjure up comforting feelings of home. The classic campfire meal in *The Lord of the Rings* is the coney stew cooked by Sam (page 156), after Gollum produces two dead rabbits for his Hobbit masters. Much to Gollum's disgust, Sam sets about using them to make a stew, for which he finds a few herbs but no stock or "taters" (potatoes). Simple as the dish is, the food seems like a feast to the half-starved Hobbits, reviving their spirits before they continue their journey into Mordor.

LUNCHEON

Lunch is a rather overlooked meal in our real world, often reduced to a quick sandwich and a cup of coffee at a desk. In the Shire, however, lunch is an important meal, as Peregrin Took is quick to point out on the Hobbits' first full day's march after leaving Hobbiton, near the beginning of The Lord of the Rings. The road may go on forever—so Bilbo is fond of pointing out—but no one, least of all the rather lazy Pippin, can do without a rest and a proper bite to eat.

WARM FIG AND PROSCIUTTO SALAD WITH BLUE CHEESE

This salad is perfect for eating al fresco on summer nights. It's just as delicious without the prosciutto if you'd prefer a vegetarian option.

Tolkien wrote that his Númenórean civilization was partly inspired by ancient Egypt. You can see that inspiration in the names of some of the Númenórean kings, such as Ar-Pharazôn, and in the "valley of the tombs" at the foot of the sacred mountain at the center of Númenor, Meneltarma, which resembles the real-world Egyptian Valley of the Kings with its elaborate royal tombs.

In honor of Númenor's spiritual connection to ancient Egypt, this dish features figs, which were popular with the Egyptians.

SERVES FOUR
PREP AND COOK 15 MINUTES

INGREDIENTS

2 tablespoons olive oil
2 banana shallots*, finely chopped
2 garlic cloves, finely chopped
2 teaspoons raspberry vinegar
8 small, ripe but firm figs
¾ cup Gorgonzola cheese, grated
2 ½ cups arugula leaves
8 wafer-thin slices of prosciutto-style ham
Salt and black pepper
Lightly crushed toasted hazelnuts

* Re-create the flavour of banana shallots by chopping 2 parts white onion and 1 part garlic for your recipe.

1 Heat the oil in a small skillet over medium-low heat. Add the shallots and garlic and fry for 4 to 5 minutes, until softened. Remove from the heat and whisk in the vinegar plus a pinch of salt and pepper.

2 Meanwhile, use a sharp knife to score a cross into the top of the figs. Press them open and fill with the Gorgonzola. Place on a baking sheet, drizzle with a little oil and slide under a preheated medium-hot broiler for 4 to 5 minutes, until melting and lightly browned.

3 Arrange the arugula, warm figs, and ham on 4 plates. Drizzle over the warm dressing and garnish with toasted hazelnuts, and a pinch of black pepper.

WALNUT, PEAR AND GREEN LEAF SALAD

The Parmesan "croûtes" make this a very elegant-looking salad, though if you are pushed for time you could simply use a vegetable peeler to shave whisper-thin slices of Parmesan over the salad just before serving.

Salad is among the many refreshments requested by the Dwarves who land unexpectedly on Bilbo's doorstep at the beginning of The Hobbit. *Salads were likely present at other meals, such as at Tom Bombadil and Goldberry's vegetarian table, and at larger feasts where all manner of foods were served. While very few characters in Tolkien's legendarium are strictly vegetarian, vegetables seem to be enjoyed with gusto by the heroes of every one of the Free Peoples, be they Man, Elf, Dwarf, or Hobbit.*

SERVES FOUR
PREP AND COOK 20 MINUTES

INGREDIENTS

¾ cup Parmesan cheese, grated
2 large ripe pears, halved, cored, and cut into thin slices
About ½ cup walnut pieces, toasted
2 ½ cups mixed salad leaves

For the dressing
¼ cup, plus 2 tablespoons walnut oil
2 tablespoons lemon juice
1 tablespoon grainy mustard
2 teaspoons superfine sugar
Several tarragon sprigs, roughly chopped

1 Oil a foil-lined baking sheet and scatter the Parmesan over it, spreading it into a thin layer about 10 inches square. Cook under a hot broiler for 2 to 3 minutes until the cheese has melted and is pale golden in color. Leave until cool enough to handle, then peel the foil away, letting the cheese break into pieces to form "croûtes."

2 Whisk together the dressing ingredients in a large bowl. Toast the walnuts.

3 Add the pears, walnuts, and salad leaves to the bowl with the dressing and toss together. Divide salad among 4 serving plates and scatter with the Parmesan croûtes.

FORAGED SALAD

For a more substantial meal, thinly slice 3 chorizo sausages diagonally and fry in a hot pan until golden and crispy. Drain on paper towels, then add to the salad.

The Rangers of the North are Men descended from the Dúnedain of the lost kingdom of Arnor who patrol its former lands and guard its remaining fragments, such as the Shire and Bree-land. When we first meet Aragorn at the beginning of The Lord of the Rings, *he is living as a Ranger, wandering Eriador, and protecting the country from Orcs and wolves. As a Ranger, Aragorn has experience living off the land, foraging for food, and in finding healing herbs, such as Athelas, or Kingsfoil. This salad makes a fresh and vibrant summer dish and uses gathered herbs like those Aragorn may have used to brighten his campfire meals.*

SERVES FOUR
PREP AND COOK 15 MINUTES

INGREDIENTS

1 cup frozen peas
1 ¼ cups fava beans
1 cup snow pea tendrils
Small handful each of mint, dill and
    parsley, finely chopped
1 cup feta cheese

For the dressing
1 teaspoon Dijon mustard
2 tablespoons olive oil
1 tablespoon chardonnay vinegar
Salt and black pepper

1 Bring a large saucepan of lightly salted water to a boil and cook the peas for 2 minutes. Refresh in cold water.

2 Cook the fava beans for 3 minutes, rinse and peel to reveal the bright green inside.

3 Mix the peas and fava beans with the snow pea tendrils and roughly chopped herbs.

4 Make the dressing by whisking the mustard, oil and vinegar together. Season to taste with salt and pepper.

5 Crumble the feta into the salad, carefully mix in the dressing and serve.

PIPPIN'S MINAS TIRITH LUNCH

Based on that British favorite—the ploughman's lunch—this is more a job of assembly rather than a recipe. Scale the quantities up or down, depending on the number of people you are feeding. Arrange the ingredients decoratively on a wooden board. Try to vary the height and color of ingredients to add visual interest. You can also add different cheeses and preserves, crackers, pâté, and seasonal fruit—whatever takes your fancy.

SERVES TWO
PREP 10 MINUTES

INGREDIENTS

4 to 6 thick slices of crusty bread or 4 Elvish White Bread Rolls (page 56)
Chunk of good-quality cheddar cheese or ripe brie
6 thick slices of cold rare roast beef or ham
2 slices of Pork Pie
2 hard-boiled eggs, peeled and halved
4 pickled onions or gherkins
2 celery stalks, preferably still with their leaves
4 radishes
2 apples, quartered and cored
Sea salt and black pepper

1 Arrange the bread or rolls in a basket.

2 Arrange the rest of the ingredients decoratively on a large wooden board, scatter salt and pepper over the eggs, and place the board in the middle of the table.

3 Spoon some of the Pickled Peaches (page 61) and the Ale, Apple and Mustard Chutney (page 65) into small bowls to serve alongside the Pork Pie (page 62) and the cold meat.

Tolkien depicts Peregrin Took as not only the youngest of the Hobbits and the most foolhardy, but also the hungriest! After Pippin has been introduced to Denethor, the Ruling Steward of Gondor, he is placed under the care of Beregond, a captain of the guard of Minas Tirith. Ever eager for his next meal, Pippin pleads for food and is given a "nuncheon" (noonday meal) of bread, butter, cheese, and apples, all washed down with a flagon of ale.

This kind of meal would have been common for farmworkers in real-world England from the 14th century onward. Popularly known as the ploughman's lunch, the traditional combination of bread, cheese, pickles, and beer was, in the 20th century, reimagined as a popular pub lunch in the United Kingdom.

HONEY-SPICED CARROT AND PARSNIP STAR

This vegetarian lunch dish is perfect with a side salad of arugula leaves lightly dressed with a tangy vinaigrette and also works well as an accompaniment to the Lake-town Beef Pot Roast on page 154. Make it vegan-friendly by using maple syrup instead of the honey.

SERVES FOUR
PREP AND COOK 50 MINUTES

INGREDIENTS

4 small parsnips, cut lengthwise into quarters
4 small carrots, cut lengthwise into quarters
3 tablespoons vegetable oil
1 teaspoon ground cumin
1 teaspoon ground coriander
½ teaspoon celery salt
3 tablespoons sweet chili sauce
1 tablespoon honey

1 Put the parsnips and carrots in a bowl.

2 In a separate small bowl or jug, mix together the oil, cumin, coriander, and celery salt. Add to the vegetables and mix well, turning until they are evenly coated.

3 Scatter in a shallow roasting pan in a single layer and place in a preheated oven, 400°F, for about 30 minutes, turning the vegetables frequently, until tender and golden.

4 Meanwhile, combine the sweet chili sauce and honey in a small bowl.

5 Brush the vegetables with the chili and honey sauce, and return to the oven for an additional 5 minutes.

6 Serve arranged on a large platter so that the widest ends of the vegetables are in the center of the dish with the tips radiating outward like the points of a star, alternating between carrots and parsnips.

Stars and Elves have a deep symbolic and poetic connection in Tolkien's work. It is Varda, Queen of the Valar, who, before the appearance of the Moon and Sun, creates a fresh set of stars in the sky to accompany the Awakening of the Elves. The Elves are consequently called the Eldar, meaning "the People of the Stars," though later the name is reserved only for those among them who undertake the Great Journey into the West.

This connection between stars and Elves continues throughout The Silmarillion. The House of Fëanor— Fëanor being the Elven creator of the Silmarils—has an eight-pointed star as its emblem, and one of the Silmarils ultimately becomes the Star of Eärendil—a divine sign of hope for the Free Peoples of Middle-earth.

This dish brings the recurring star motif from Tolkien's work to your dining table.

ROASTED STUFFED PEPPER FLAMES

Serve these as a light lunch with crusty bread or as a side dish to
Rosemary Lamb Skewers (page 150). It's very versatile—try adding a few
sliced black olives, some crumbled feta, or chunks of Halloumi cheese.

*The Balrogs of Middle-earth are Maiar—angelic beings—corrupted by Morgoth, not unlike
the fallen angels that were cast down from heaven with Lucifer in Christian theology. These
terrifying beings cloak themselves in shadow and flame, arm themselves with swords and
whips, and pose a great threat to the Free Peoples of Middle-earth. The Silmarillion and The
Lord of the Rings both feature dramatic battles with Balrogs. In The Silmarillion the Balrog
Gothmog is slain by the Elf-lord Ecthelion in the battle for Gondolin, and in The Fellowship
of the Ring Gandalf defeats a Balrog named Durin's Bane in the mines of Moria, though he
himself "dies" in the battle.*

*These stuffed red peppers are shaped like the bright red flames that give the Balrogs their
physical form. Fortunately, these flames are harbingers of deliciousness rather than of doom
and destruction.*

SERVES TWO
PREP AND COOK I HOUR 10 MINUTES

INGREDIENTS

4 large red Romano chili peppers, halved
    lengthwise, cored, and deseeded
2 garlic cloves, crushed
1 ½ tablespoons chopped thyme
4 plum tomatoes, diced
4 tablespoons extra virgin olive oil
2 tablespoons balsamic vinegar
Salt and black pepper

1 Put the pepper halves, cut-side up, in a
roasting pan lined with foil or in a ceramic
dish. Divide the garlic and thyme between
them and season with salt and pepper. Split
the diced tomato evenly between the pepper
halves and drizzle with the oil and vinegar.

2 Roast in a preheated oven, 425°F, for about
1 hour until the peppers are soft and charred.

3 For a fiery effect, arrange on a dark-colored
platter with the wide bases of the "flames" on
one end and the fiery points licking upward.

THE PRANCING PONY'S POTATO AND GARLIC SOUP

A mug of this hearty potato soup, with its enticing aroma of smoked garlic, is just the thing to wrap chilled hands around on a blustery day. Serve it with some Elvish White Bread Rolls (page 56) for a filling meal.

After a long day's journey through the Barrow-downs, the roaring fire and pints of ale at The Prancing Pony in Bree reinvigorate the weary, scared party of Hobbits. We like to think that one of the foods waiting to greet weary travelers at this venerable Arnorian institution would have been a comforting bowl of hot soup. Perhaps the soup of the day at The Pony changed with the seasons, but this might well have been one of its more popular winter warmers.

SERVES FOUR
PREP AND COOK 50 MINUTES

INGREDIENTS

4 tablespoons unsalted butter
1 large onion, sliced
2 garlic cloves, crushed
3 ¾ cups floury potatoes, peeled and
  cut into small cubes
3 ½ cups vegetable stock
½ teaspoon smoked sea salt
½ cup milk
4 tablespoons fresh herbs, such as
  parsley, thyme and chives
Snipped chives to garnish
Black pepper

1 Melt the butter in a large saucepan, add the onion and garlic, and cook over medium heat for 3 to 4 minutes until softened. Stir in the potatoes, cover, and cook for 5 minutes.

2 Add the stock and season. Bring to a boil, then reduce the heat, cover, and simmer for 30 minutes until the potatoes are tender.

3 Transfer to a food processor and blend until smooth. Return to the pan, stir in the milk and herbs, and reheat gently. Serve garnished with snipped chives and black pepper.

Following Page:
The Barrow-downs

THE SOUP OF STORY

This soup makes good use of all the odds and ends you may have lying around—you can experiment with different flavors by adding whatever you have on hand. If you'd prefer a chunkier version of this fresh-tasting soup, don't blend it and, if you like, stir through a dollop of pesto (page 95) before serving. To keep it vegan, leave out the crème fraîche.

Tolkien had a striking metaphor for thinking about how storytelling draws on a wide range of influences. In one of his letters, he compares an author inventing a story to someone making a soup. An author's story is made up of a hodgepodge of all sorts of memories and odds and ends of knowledge, mixed together and blended into something astonishing and new. Even if some of the ingredients can be identified, the ingredients are less important to the soup—or story—than the final flavor.

SERVES FOUR
PREP AND COOK 40 MINUTES

INGREDIENTS

1 teaspoon olive oil
1 leek, finely sliced
1 large potato, peeled and chopped
3 ½ cups vegetable stock
2 cups mixed summer vegetables (such as peas, asparagus, fava beans, and zucchini)
2 tablespoons chopped mint
2 tablespoons crème fraîche (optional), to serve
Salt and black pepper

1 Heat the oil in a medium saucepan and fry the leek for
   3 to 4 minutes until softened.

2 Add the potato and stock to the pan and cook for
   10 minutes. Add all of the remaining vegetables and the
   mint, then bring to a boil. Reduce the heat and simmer
   for 10 minutes.

3 Transfer the soup to a blender or food processor and blend
   until smooth. Return the soup to the pan, add the crème
   fraîche, if using, and season to taste with salt and pepper.
   Heat through gently and serve with a warm flatbread.

GOLLUM'S RAW FISH

Ask your fishmonger for "sushi-grade" salmon for the best (and safest) results. You could also use smoked salmon for this recipe.

Gollum mentions fish rather often in Tolkien's books—they're the answer to one of the riddles he poses to Bilbo in The Hobbit *and he mentions his love for fish when talking about food with Sam on their journey to Mordor. He's very clear, however, that cooking any food—meat or fish— "ruins" it.*

Raw fish, properly prepared, does have a wonderful and delicate flavor when it is very fresh. This recipe takes its inspiration from Japanese cuisine for a fresh tasty dish that just might convince you that Gollum has a point.

SERVES TWO TO THREE
PREP <u>AND</u> **COOK** 50 MINUTES, PLUS
COOLING

INGREDIENTS

Good 1 ½ cups sushi rice
6 tablespoons rice wine vinegar
2 ½ tablespoons superfine sugar
1 ½ pickled ginger, chopped
½ teaspoon wasabi paste
½ cucumber
½ pound skinless salmon, cut into bite-
   sized pieces
1 avocado, peeled, pitted and cut into
   small cubes
8 scallions, finely sliced
3 tablespoons toasted sesame seeds,
   to garnish

1   Cook the rice according to instructions on
    the package.

2   Meanwhile, put the vinegar and sugar in a
    small saucepan and heat gently, stirring, to
    dissolve the sugar. Turn off the heat, add the
    pickled ginger and wasabi, and leave to cool.

3   Cut the cucumber in half lengthwise and
    scoop out the seeds. Slice the flesh finely and
    add to the cooled vinegar mix.

4   When the rice is cooked, transfer it to a dish,
    strain the vinegar mixture over it, reserving
    the cucumber, stir and leave to cool.

5   Transfer the cooled rice to a large salad bowl
    and combine gently with the cucumber,
    salmon, avocado, and scallions. Top with
    toasted sesame seeds and serve.

Gollum and his fish

EASTERLING TEA-MARINATED TROUT

Kecap manis is an Indonesian sweet soy sauce with a taste that has a hint of molasses. If you don't have Kecap manis, you can use ordinary soy sauce, but add a little more honey to the marinade to balance the flavors.

In Tolkien, the name Easterlings is usually given to the peoples of Rhûn, the vast territories in the east of Middle-earth, encompassing both nomadic tribes, such as the Wainriders, and more settled folk, such as the Balchoth. Tolkien provides only vague sketches of these remote cultures—which by the time of the War of the Ring are largely in thrall to Sauron and to the land of Mordor.

This recipe brings in ingredients from the real-world East to help you imagine the world of the Easterlings beyond the page.

SERVES FOUR

PREP AND COOK 25 MINUTES, PLUS INFUSING, COOLING AND MARINATING 4 ½ HOURS

INGREDIENTS

- 2 black tea bags (such as Lapsang souchong) infused in 7 ounces boiling water
- 1 tablespoon peeled and grated ginger
- 1 garlic clove, crushed
- 4 tablespoons Kecap manis
- 2 tablespoons sweet chili sauce
- 1 tablespoon honey
- 4 trout fillets, about 3 ½ ounces each
- 1 tablespoon sesame oil
- 2 tablespoons peanut oil, divided use
- 2 ½ cups baby bok choy, halved lengthwise

1 Once the tea bags have infused for 5 minutes, discard the bags. Stir in the ginger, garlic, Kecap manis, sweet chili sauce, and honey until well blended. Leave to cool.

2 Lay the trout fillets in a shallow nonmetallic dish and pour over the tea mixture. Cover and leave to marinate in the refrigerator for at least 4 hours, or overnight if time permits, turning the fish occasionally.

3 Remove the fish, reserving the marinade, and pat dry on paper towels.

4 Heat the sesame oil with 1 tablespoon of the peanut oil in a large nonstick skillet, add the fish, skin-side down, and cook for 2 to 3 minutes. Turn the fish over and cook for 3 minutes. Remove to a warmed plate and cover with foil—it will continue cooking in its own steam while you cook the bok choy.

5 Heat the remaining oil in the skillet over high heat, add the bok choy and stir-fry until just beginning to wilt. Pour in half the reserved marinade, bring to a boil and cook for 3 to 4 minutes until most of the liquid has evaporated and the bok choy is tender. Serve with the trout.

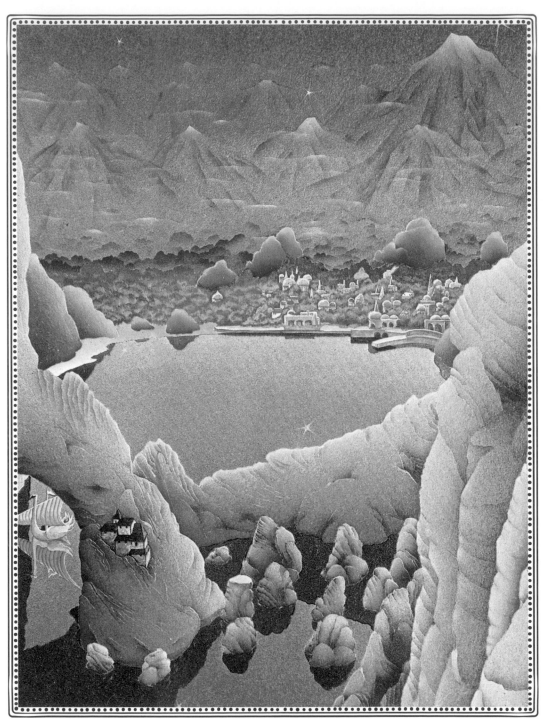

The Swan Haven of Alqualondë

ALQUALONDËAN GRILLED SCALLOPS WITH PESTO

Grilling sea scallops on a hot barbecue or seared in a hot pan until they have a light golden color will enhance their mild, sweet flavor, but take care not to overcook them as this will make them chewy.

Alqualondë is the great Elven city built by the Teleri—one of the three kindreds of the Eldar—on the coast of Valinor. Its very name seems to conjure up a watery paradise. Tolkien tells us the Teleri spend their days diving for pearls, so we might easily imagine them catching the odd scallop as well!

Bring Alqualondë-inspired elegance to your dinner table with these beautiful scallops served in the shell. These beautiful appetizers are surprisingly easy to make and will be the highlight of any lunch or dinner gathering.

SERVES FOUR
PREP AND COOK 20 MINUTES

INGREDIENTS

12 sea scallops on the half shell
(if unavailable, use without the shell)
Olive oil, for drizzling and frying

For the pesto
2 ½ cups basil
1 garlic clove, crushed
2 tablespoons pine nuts, toasted
¼ teaspoon sea salt
⅓ cup, plus 1 tablespoon extra virgin olive oil
2 tablespoons grated Parmesan cheese
Black pepper

1 Make the pesto. Place the basil, garlic, pine nuts, and sea salt in a mortar and grind with a pestle to form a fairly smooth paste. Slowly add the oil until you reach the required texture (soft but not runny), then finally add the cheese and pepper, to taste.

2 Season the scallops lightly with pepper. Drizzle with a little oil and grill, shell-side down, on a hot barbecue for 3 to 4 minutes until cooked. (They will cook through the shell.) Alternatively, heat 1 tablespoon of olive oil in a large skillet. Pat the scallops dry with paper towels, season with salt, and then fry for 2 to 3 minutes on each side until golden and just cooked through.

3 Serve topped with a spoonful of the pesto.

GREY HAVENS GARLICKY GRILLED MUSSELS

When buying mussels, look for ones with tightly closed shells that feel heavy. Store them loosely wrapped rather than in a sealed container so that they can breathe—they're best eaten the same day you buy them.

The sea plays little role in the largely landlocked tales of The Hobbit *and* The Lord of the Rings. *Thus, when it finally makes an appearance at the end of* The Return of the King, *with the departure of the Ring-bearers, including Frodo, from the Grey Havens over the Sundering Sea, it has all the more emotive power. It is as if all our horizons have suddenly opened, dazzling and wide. We might imagine this dish as the meal enjoyed by the party of Elves, Hobbits, and the Wizard as they bade farewell to Middle-earth.*

SERVES FOUR
PREP AND COOK 30 MINUTES

INGREDIENTS

½ cup butter
2 shallots, chopped
3 garlic cloves, chopped, divided use
½ cup dry white wine
1 pound 6 ounces mussels, debearded and scrubbed
1 cup coarse bread crumbs
2 tablespoons finely chopped parsley
1 teaspoon finely grated lemon zest
2 tablespoons grated Parmesan cheese
1 tablespoon olive oil

1 Melt the butter in a large saucepan over medium-low heat and cook the shallots and 2 of the garlic cloves for 5 to 6 minutes until softened. Add the wine and bring to a boil.

2 Add the mussels to the pan, discarding any that won't close when sharply tapped, then cover and simmer gently for 3 to 5 minutes, shaking the pan occasionally until the shells are opened. Discard any that remain closed. Set aside.

3 Put the bread crumbs in a bowl with the parsley, remaining garlic, lemon zest, Parmesan, and oil and mix well.

4 Discard the empty half-shell from each mussel and arrange the mussels in a single layer on a large baking sheet.

5 Spoon the bread crumb mixture neatly over the mussels and slide under a preheated medium broiler for 2 to 3 minutes, or until the bread crumbs are crisp and golden.

UMBRIAN SHRIMP AND MONKFISH SKEWERS

Give your fish even more flavor by replacing the usual wooden or metal skewers with sturdy rosemary sprigs that will impart a lovely herbal scent and look pretty, too. It's important to soak them well before using so they don't burn and ruin the fish.

The Corsairs of Umbar are sworn enemies of Gondor throughout the Third Age, pillaging and terrorizing its southern coasts with their pirate fleets. The Corsairs appear in The Lord of the Rings *when Aragorn captures their ships and rows them to Minas Tirith with reinforcements during the Battle of the Pelennor Fields.*

The city of Umbar itself lies on the Bay of Belfalas, in the Near Harad, and these simple kebabs of shrimp and pieces of monkfish may well be similar to something the Corsairs might have made to fuel their pillaging expeditions along Gondor's rugged coastline.

SERVES FOUR

PREP AND COOK 20 MINUTES, PLUS SOAKING AND MARINATING 1 ½ HOURS

INGREDIENTS

8 large rosemary sprigs
1 pound monkfish fillets, cut into 16 large chunks
16 raw peeled tiger shrimp, deveined
2 garlic cloves, crushed
Grated zest and juice of 1 lemon, divided use
1 ½ tablespoons extra virgin olive oil
Salt and black pepper

For the lemon aïoli

3 egg yolks
2 teaspoons white wine vinegar
1 teaspoon Dijon mustard
2 to 4 garlic cloves, crushed
1 tablespoon lemon juice
1 cup extra virgin olive oil
Salt and white pepper

1   Remove the rosemary leaves from the stalks and set aside, leaving a few rosemary leaves on the end of each sprig, and cut the other end on a diagonal to form a sharp tip. Soak in cold water for 30 minutes. Finely chop 1 tablespoon of the rosemary leaves, reserving the rest for another dish.

2   Thread the fish chunks on to the soaked rosemary skewers, alternating with the shrimp, allowing 2 cubes of fish and 2 shrimp per skewer. Place in a shallow nonmetallic dish.

3   Combine the chopped rosemary, garlic, lemon zest, and some salt and black pepper with the oil, pour over the kebabs and leave to marinate for 1 hour.

4   Make the aïoli. Place the egg yolks, vinegar, mustard, garlic, lemon juice, and a little salt and white pepper in a food processor, and blend briefly until the egg mixture is frothy. Then, with the blade running, gradually pour in the oil through the funnel until the sauce is thick and glossy. Thin with a little boiling water if it gets too thick. Adjust the seasoning to taste.

5   Remove the kebabs from the marinade. Grill on a hot barbecue for 2 to 3 minutes on each side until cooked. Alternatively, cook under a preheated hot broiler for 2 to 3 minutes on each side.

6   Squeeze the lemon juice over the kebabs and serve with the lemon aïoli.

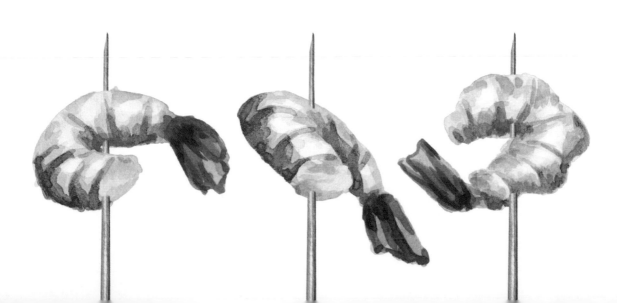

MIRKWOOD BATWINGS

Black food gel makes these "bat wings" a convincingly dark and scary hue, but for something a little less frightening you can simply omit the food coloring and still enjoy the Asian-inspired flavors of this dish.

As Bilbo and the Dwarves learned the hard way in The Hobbit, *if you light a fire in Mirkwood at night you will immediately attract thousands of moths with huge black bats hot on their trail. However, we like to think you can use this to your advantage if your supplies have otherwise run low and you catch a few for your dinner. When marinated and roasted, your "bat wings" will be crispy and delectable.*

SERVES FOUR

PREP AND COOK 20 MINUTES, PLUS MARINATING 1 TO 2 HOURS

INGREDIENTS

8 large chicken wings, about 3 ½ ounces each

For the marinade
1 garlic clove
2-inch piece of ginger, peeled and chopped
Juice and finely grated zest of 2 limes
2 tablespoons dark soy sauce
2 tablespoons peanut oil
2 teaspoons ground cinnamon
1 teaspoon ground turmeric
2 tablespoons honey
3 drops of black food gel
Salt

1   Soak 8 bamboo skewers in cold water
    for 30 minutes.

2   Place the marinade ingredients in a
    blender or food processor and blend
    until smooth.

3   Arrange the chicken wings in a shallow
    nonmetallic dish, pour the marinade
    over and toss to cover. Cover and leave
    to marinate for 1 to 2 hours.

4   Remove the chicken from the
    marinade, thread on to the skewers
    and grill on a hot barbecue for
    4 to 5 minutes on each side, basting
    with the remaining marinade.
    Alternatively, cook under a preheated
    hot broiler for 4 to 5 minutes on
    each side, basting with the remaining
    marinade.

Mirkwood

NONTRADITIONAL DIETS IN MIDDLE-EARTH

The vast majority of the peoples of Middle-earth—Men, Elves, and Hobbits—eat a fairly conventional diet—the meat, vegetables, and grains that would have gone unremarked in Europe from the Middle Ages on. A few post-medieval European staples—such as sugar and tomatoes—may be famously missing, but some are notoriously present, such as potatoes, tea, coffee, and pipeweed (tobacco).

However, there are some more unusual diets in Middle-earth. Tom Bombadil and his wife, Goldberry, appear to be vegetarian. When they shelter Frodo, Sam, Merry, and Pippin after their ordeal in the Old Forest, they lay the table with cream, honeycomb, and white bread, butter, cheese, and milk, and "green herbs and ripe berries gathered"—all foods that suggest the diet of slightly hippyish smallholders, the produce of whose dairy and vegetable patch are supplemented by foraging. To drink, the couple offer what appears to be fresh, clear water but whose effect is as heady and merrymaking as wine. As Bombadil and Goldberry bear similarities to nature spirits, we might imagine their vegetarianism to be ethically based—they have an affinity with living things. Another ethical vegetarian is the hero Beren in *The Silmarillion*, who while living in the wild is befriended by animals. The Ents perhaps have the most eco-friendly diet, nourished solely by a miraculous brew that consists of little more than river water.

At the other end of the ethical spectrum are the Orcs—or Goblins, as they are known in *The Hobbit*—whose diet seems to consist largely of raw meat, including that of horses and ponies, and a rough-tasting liquor (page 166) of the kind intermittently poured down the throats of Merry and Pippin after their kidnapping. There are suggestions that the Uruk-hai—a kind of super-breed of Orcs—eat Men's flesh and that they even practice a kind of cannibalism, dining on the flesh of their lesser kindred.

Meanwhile, Gollum, that most Orc-like of Hobbits, supplements his raw meat diet with the occasional blind fish. He expresses disgust at the idea of cooking anything and even of eating "grasses" (herbs) and roots—he would only resort to such a repulsive thing, he tells Sam, if he were starving. As one doctor has pointed out in a carefully researched paper, both the light-shunning Orcs and Gollum would have suffered from a debilitating lack of vitamin D.

AFTERNOON TEA

There is something quintessentially Hobbitish about afternoon tea—it is hard to imagine the rugged Men of Gondor, let alone the Elves of Rivendell or Lothlórien, stopping to partake in something quite so self-indulgent... and so absolutely delicious! That said, if Bilbo's "unexpected party"—which at least begins as an afternoon tea—is anything to go by, Dwarves are more than partial to a cake or several, while Thorin and Company's encounter with Beorn the Beorning reveal him, too, to be a skilled baker!

BEET TARTE TATIN
WITH GOAT CHEESE

This showstopper looks smart but is simple to make. Try to cut the beets into equal pieces and arrange in a single, compact layer in an attractive way as they will be at the top when you serve the tarte tatin.

The humble beet is an under-celebrated vegetable, but, like the unassuming Hobbits of the Shire, it can be elevated to greatness under the right conditions. Rich, filling and with a touch of creamy tanginess, we think this ruby-red tarte is a gem that would've been fit for Elrond's table in the Last Homely House.

SERVES FOUR TO SIX
PREP AND COOK 45 MINUTES

INGREDIENTS

2 tablespoons olive oil
2 garlic cloves, chopped
1 teaspoon thyme leaves
2 tablespoons balsamic vinegar
6 medium cooked beets (not pickled),
   sliced or cut into thin wedges
8 ounces ready-made chilled puff pastry
All-purpose flour, for dusting
½ cup crumbly goat cheese
Thyme leaves or snipped chives, to
   garnish

1 Place the oil in an ovenproof skilllet over medium-low heat and, when hot, fry the garlic and thyme for 1 to 2 minutes until just softened. Pour in the vinegar and simmer gently for 1 to 2 minutes until just sticky.

2 Arrange the beets to fit snugly and attractively in the pan, then increase the heat slightly and cook for 4 to 5 minutes until the underside begins to brown.

3 Meanwhile, place the pastry on a floured work surface and roll into a circle about ½ inch larger than the skillet.

4 Lay the pastry over the skillet, tucking the edges in neatly to cover the beets, and bake in a preheated oven, 400°F, for 15 to 20 minutes until the pastry is puffed and golden.

5 Invert the tarte on to a large plate, then crumble the goat cheese over, and serve garnished with the thyme or chives.

WARM MUSHROOM CROSTINI

These light and savory little mushroom toasts are a lovely alternative to sweet teatime treats. Tarragon and mushroom are a classic pairing but you could use parsley or marjoram instead of tarragon.

Mushrooms are dearly loved by Hobbits, especially by Frodo, who as a young lad steals mushrooms from Farmer Maggot's fields. Mushrooms hide in plain sight, blending into the woodland or meadow floor, just as Hobbits blend into their native landscape, having the natural ability to make themselves go unseen by ordinary folks if they see fit. Perhaps this shared capacity to disappear into the landscape is what inspired Tolkien to make Hobbits so fond of mushrooms.

SERVES FOUR
PREP AND COOK 15 MINUTES

INGREDIENTS

6 tablespoons butter
2 garlic cloves, 1 chopped and 1 left whole
1 tablespoon chopped tarragon
3 cups roughly chopped cremini or portobello mushrooms
Sea salt and freshly ground black pepper
1 tablespoon olive oil
Sourdough or country-style bread, thinly sliced

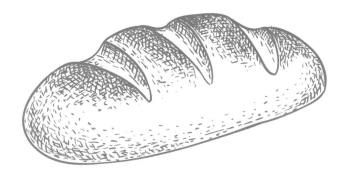

1   Melt the butter in a large skillet. Add the chopped garlic and tarragon and heat until the butter just begins to foam.

2   Add the chopped mushrooms to the pan and fry over medium heat for 4 to 5 minutes until soft and golden. Generously season with salt and pepper.

3   Meanwhile, lightly brush each slice of bread with a little olive oil. Heat a ridged grill pan and when hot, toast the bread until golden and nicely charred.

4   Once toasted, rub each piece of toast lightly with the whole garlic clove.

5   Arrange the crostini on 4 plates, spoon over the buttery mushrooms and serve immediately.

BILBO'S SEED-CAKE

Seed-cake is distinctively flavored with caraway seeds. This version has a citrus spin and makes for an elegant and understated teatime treat. Any slightly stale cake left over gives you the perfect excuse to use it up in a trifle.

SERVES TEN
PREP AND COOK 1 ½ HOURS

INGREDIENTS

¾ cup butter, at room temperature
1 cup superfine sugar
3 eggs, beaten
Scant 2 cups self-rising flour
1 teaspoon baking powder
1 ½ teaspoons roughly crushed caraway seeds
Grated zest of 1 large orange and 5 to 6 tablespoons orange juice
⅛ cup granulated sugar

1 Grease and line a 2-pound loaf pan.

2 Beat the butter and superfine sugar together in a mixing bowl until pale and creamy. Gradually mix in alternate spoonfuls of beaten egg and flour until all has been added and the mixture is smooth. Stir in the baking powder, caraway seeds, orange zest, and juice, to make a soft dropping consistency.

3 Spoon the mixture into the prepared loaf pan. Spread the surface level and sprinkle with the granulated sugar.

4 Bake in a preheated oven, 325°F, for 1 hour to 1 hour 10 minutes until well risen, the top is cracked and golden, and a skewer inserted into the center comes out clean.

5 Leave to cool in the pan for 10 minutes, then loosen the edges and lift out of the pan using the lining paper. Transfer to a wire rack, peel off the lining paper, and leave to cool. Store in an airtight tin for up to 1 week.

At the beginning of The Hobbit, *one of his unexpected visitors, Balin—a very old-looking Dwarf—asks, very specifically, for seed-cake. Bilbo has baked a couple of seed-cakes only that afternoon and so he is able to oblige, if unwillingly—his plan was to eat them as an after-supper treat. Seed-cake is a style of cake that was popular in England through the Victorian era and into the early 1900s, which is the period that Tolkien is fondly remembering when he describes the foods of the Shire.*

Bilbo Baggins

NIPHREDIL SHORTBREAD COOKIES

These dainty, buttery cookies with their delicate flower pattern are perfect for a special-occasion tea party. Keep for up to a week in an airtight tin.

These charming cookies are inspired by the small white flowers that originally grew in the footsteps of Lúthien, the Elven princess of the woodland kingdom of Doriath in Beleriand. In the Second and Third Ages, the flower also blossoms in Lothlórien, where, as long as Galadriel rules there, it is perpetually spring. Both Lúthien and Galadriel are reminiscent of the White Ladies of Welsh mythology— otherworldly figures who rule over beguiling forest realms.

MAKES FOURTEEN
PREP AND COOK 40 MINUTES

INGREDIENTS

1 ⅓ cups all-purpose flour, plus extra
  for dusting
½ cup ground almonds
¼ cup superfine sugar, plus extra,
  to decorate
A few drops of almond extract
1 ¼ sticks butter, diced

To decorate
⅕ cup whole blanched almonds, halved
2 candied cherries, cut into small pieces

1   Put the flour, ground almonds, sugar, and almond extract in a mixing bowl or a food processor. Add the butter and rub in with your fingertips or process until the mixture resembles fine bread crumbs.

2   Squeeze the mixture together with your hands to form a ball. Knead lightly, then roll out on a lightly floured surface until ½-inch thick. Stamp out 2 ½-inch circles using a fluted round cookie cutter. Transfer to an ungreased baking sheet. Re-knead the trimmings and continue rolling and stamping out until all of the mixture has been used.

3   Prick each shortbread cookie 4 times with a fork to make a star shape then add an almond half to the space between each fork mark to make a small white flower. Decorate the center with a small piece of candied cherry. Sprinkle with a little extra superfine sugar and bake in a preheated oven, 325°F, for about 15 minutes until pale golden.

4   Transfer the cookies to a wire rack to cool before serving.

STRAWBERRY AND LAVENDER SHORTCAKES

The scents and tastes of summer come together in edible form in these gorgeous shortcakes. They are best eaten on the day they are filled, but the plain cookies can be stored in an airtight tin for up to 3 days.

Nothing evokes the bliss of summer better than strawberries and cream, and it is to strawberries and cream that Tolkien turns when he imagines the "eucatastrophe" (happy catastrophe) with which—save for the departure of the Ring-bearers— The Lord of the Rings closes. During the miraculous year of 1420 (Shire Reckoning)—a time of bumper harvests in the Shire, in part at least due to Sam's ministrations—the young Hobbits are said to be almost floating in strawberries and cream!

These strawberry and lavender shortcakes embrace the abundance of strawberries and cream born from a good season. They make a delightful sweet course for tea or a charming summer dessert.

MAKES EIGHT
PREP AND COOK 40 MINUTES

INGREDIENTS

Generous 1 cup all-purpose flour, plus
   extra for dusting
⅛ cup ground rice
½ cup butter, diced
¼ cup superfine sugar
1 tablespoon lavender petals

To decorate

1 ½ cups strawberries (or a mixture of
   strawberries and raspberries)
½ cup heavy cream
16 small lavender sprigs (optional)
Sifted confectioners' sugar, for dusting

1 Put the flour and ground rice in a mixing bowl or a food processor. Add the butter and rub in with your fingertips or process until the mixture resembles fine bread crumbs.

2 Stir in the sugar and lavender petals, and squeeze the crumbs together with your hands to form a smooth ball.

3 Knead lightly then roll out on a lightly floured surface until ¼-inch thick. Stamp out 3-inch circles using a fluted round cookie cutter. Transfer to an ungreased baking sheet. Re-knead the trimmings and continue rolling and stamping until you have made 16 cookies.

4 Prick with a fork, bake in a preheated oven, 325°F, for 10 to 12 minutes until pale golden. Leave to cool on the baking sheet.

5 To serve, halve 4 of the smallest strawberries, hull and slice the rest. Whip the cream and spoon over 8 of the cookies. Top with the sliced strawberries, then the remaining cookies. Spoon the remaining cream on top and decorate with the reserved halved strawberries and tiny sprigs of lavender, if desired. Dust lightly with sifted confectioners' sugar.

BEORN'S TWICE-BAKED CAKES

As biscotti are dry, they are traditionally served with something to dunk them in. Enjoy these honey and pistachio biscotti with strong coffee, Athelas Tea (page 162) or, Italian-style, after dinner with a glass of Marsala.

In addition to the honey cakes Beorn gives to Bilbo's party for their dinner (see Beorn's Honey Cakes on page 28), Beorn also gives them twice-baked honey cakes for them to take on the road. We imagine these would have been a little bit like biscotti or hardtack—cooked twice to make them a bit crunchier, longer-lasting, and easier to carry on a journey.

MAKES APPROX. TWENTY-FOUR

PREP AND COOK 60 MINUTES, PLUS COOLING

INGREDIENTS

2 tablespoons unsalted butter, softened
¼ cup superfine sugar
Finely grated zest of 1 lemon
Scant 1 cup self-rising flour
½ teaspoon baking powder
1 tablespoon honey
1 egg yolk
1 tablespoon egg white
½ cup shelled pistachios, skinned and roughly chopped

1 Beat the butter, sugar, and lemon zest in a bowl until pale and fluffy. Sift in the flour and baking powder, then add the honey, egg yolk and white, and pistachios. Mix to a soft dough.

2 Divide the dough into 2 pieces and shape each into a sausage about 6 inches long. Place the pieces, well spaced apart, on a greased baking sheet, and flatten each to a depth of ½ inch.

3 Bake in a preheated oven, 325°F, for 20 minutes until risen and turning pale golden.

4 Remove from the oven and leave to cool for 10 minutes, leaving the oven on. Using a serrated knife, cut each sausage into ½ inch thick slices. Return to the oven, cut-sides up, for an additional 10 minutes to crisp up. Transfer to a wire rack to cool.

"DUMBLEDOR" BLUEBERRY AND HONEY JELLY

This recipe combines the delights of summer berries with the rich sweetness of honey in a jelly to enjoy all year round. Serve with Whole-wheat Molasses Scones (page 122) or spread lavishly on toast.

In Middle-earth, honey seems to be the sweetener of choice, just as it was in the medieval world. One of the characters, the skin-changer Beorn, is a keen beekeeper, and the foods he makes and serves to his guests are often enriched with honey. Honey is also included in the food served to the Hobbits by Tom Bombadil and Goldberry. The long Hobbit poem Errantry, *composed by Bilbo and collected in the* Red Book, *alludes to a kind of monster-bee called the Dumbledor, a word derived from an old English word for bumblebee.*

MAKES TWO TO THREE JARS
PREP AND COOK 35 MINUTES

INGREDIENTS

3 cups blueberries
½ cup water
Scant 2 cups gelling sugar with pectin, warmed
⅓ cup honey
Juice of 1 lemon
1 tablespoon butter (optional)

1 Add the blueberries and water to a stainless-steel jam pan and cook gently for 10 minutes until softened, crushing from time to time with a wooden spoon.

2 Add the sugar, honey, and lemon juice and heat gently, stirring from time to time, until dissolved. Bring to a boil, then boil rapidly until setting point is reached (10 to 15 minutes).

3 If there is scum on the top of the jelly, skim it off with a slotted spoon or stir in the butter to disperse it.

4 Ladle into warm, dry, sterilized jars, filling to the very top. Cover with screw-top lids, or with waxed discs and cellophane tops secured with elastic bands. Label and leave to cool.

SPICED PLUM JELLY

This jelly, with its flavor of Christmas spices, makes a great edible gift. Top each jar with a pretty square of cloth tied with a coordinating ribbon and add a gift label with some serving suggestions.

> *At the end of* The Lord of the Rings, *Tolkien describes the year following the end of the War of the Ring—1420 in the Shire Reckoning—as a time of golden plenty. In terms that may remind us of the carnivalesque paintings of the Netherlandish painter Hieronymus Bosch, he evokes—among other things—young Hobbits who are virtually swimming in strawberries and cream, or who sit under plum trees stuffing themselves with ripe fruit until they have made little pyramids of the discarded stones.*

MAKES FOUR TO FIVE JARS
PREP AND COOK 1 ¼ HOURS

INGREDIENTS

3 pounds just-ripe plums, halved and stoned
Grated zest and juice of 1 orange
1 cup water
1 cinnamon stick, halved
1 teaspoon whole cloves
7 ½ cups granulated sugar, warmed
1 tablespoon butter (optional)

Previous Page:
Great Smials

1 Add the plums, orange zest, and juice, and water to a preserving pan. Tie the cinnamon stick and cloves in muslin, then add to the preserving pan. Cover and cook gently for 30 minutes until the plums are softened.

2 Pour the sugar into the pan and heat gently, stirring occasionally, until dissolved. Bring to a boil, then boil rapidly until setting point is reached (20 to 25 minutes). If there is scum on the top of the jelly, skim it off with a slotted spoon or stir in the butter to disperse it.

3 Discard the bag of spices.

4 Ladle into warm, dry, sterilized jars, filling to the very top. Cover with screw-top lids, or with waxed discs and cellophane tops secured with elastic bands. Label and leave to cool.

STUFFED "BUCKLEBURY FERRY" PEARS

Packed with healthy fruit and nuts, this easy, low-fat dessert is perfect to finish off a fall midweek meal. You can vary the recipe by using honey in place of the maple syrup and dates to replace the prunes.

The Bucklebury Ferry carries Frodo, Sam, Merry, and Pippin across the Brandywine river into Buckland, narrowly escaping the mysterious dark horse rider who is hot on their heels. Inspired by the Bucklebury Ferry, these stuffed pears carry a delicious morsel of hazelnuts and fruit, and are served with a pool of sweet juice, just like the little ferry carrying the Hobbits across the Shire's great river.

SERVES FOUR
PREP AND COOK 45 MINUTES

INGREDIENTS

4 ripe pears, preferably a pale-skinned variety
3 ready-to-eat pitted prunes, roughly chopped
⅓ cup roasted hazelnuts, roughly chopped
½ teaspoon ground cinnamon
¼ cup maple syrup
½ cup blackberries, halved
2 tablespoons butter
Ice cream or yogurt (optional)

1 Halve the pears and then scoop a small slice from the back of each of each so that they sit level in a roasting pan. Scoop out the core and seeds, leaving the stalk intact.

2 Mix the prunes and hazelnuts with the cinnamon and maple syrup in a bowl, then fold in the blackberries. Pile into the pear cavities and top each with a ½ tablespoon of butter. Cover the roasting pan with foil and bake in a preheated oven, 400°F, for 25 minutes. Remove the foil and roast for an additional 10 minutes.

3 Serve with the juices spooned over and around the pears along with a scoop of ice cream or yogurt, if desired.

WHOLE-WHEAT MOLASSES SCONES

Serve these scones warm or cold, split, and topped with crème fraîche or thick cream and "Dumbledor" Blueberry and Honey Jelly (page 117) or Spiced Plum Jelly (page 120). They are best eaten on the day they are made.

Scones among the many delicious foods that Bilbo serves to Thorin and Company when they stumble into Bag End at the beginning of The Hobbit. *This recipe makes 14 delicious scones—enough for all 13 Dwarves, plus one left over for a late Wizard, and the perfect teatime treat when sliced in half and topped with heaps of cream and jelly. You might choose to serve them as Bilbo did, accompanied by a big pot of piping-hot coffee.*

MAKES FOURTEEN
PREP AND COOK 30 MINUTES

INGREDIENTS

3 cups whole-wheat bread flour, plus
   extra for dusting and sprinkling
   (optional)
¼ cup butter, diced
About ¼ cup light brown sugar
3 teaspoons baking powder
1 teaspoon baking soda
½ cup plain yogurt
2 tablespoons blackstrap molasses
1 egg, beaten

1   Put the flour in a mixing bowl or a food
    processor. Add the butter and rub in with
    your fingertips or process until the mixture
    resembles fine bread crumbs. Stir in the sugar
    and baking powder.

2   Stir the baking soda into the yogurt, then
    add to the flour mixture with the blackstrap
    molasses. Gradually mix in enough of the
    beaten egg to form a soft but not sticky
    dough.

3   Knead lightly, then roll out on a lightly
    floured surface until ¾-inch thick. Working
    quickly, cut out 2-inch circles using a plain
    cookie cutter. Transfer to a greased baking
    sheet. Re-knead the trimmings and continue
    rolling and stamping out until all the mixture
    has been used.

4   Add to the baking sheet and sprinkle the
    tops with a little extra flour or leave plain,
    if desired. Bake in a preheated oven, 425°F,
    for 6 to 8 minutes until well risen and
    browned.

BIFUR'S JELLY AND APPLE PIE

These individual open pies look really impressive but are easy to make. They are best served warm with a splash of cream or some crème fraîche, and are also lovely with vanilla ice cream as a dessert.

Bifur is yet another of the 13 Dwarves of Thorin and Company who show up unexpectedly at Bilbo's door at the beginning of The Hobbit. *His request is for jelly and apple pie, which Bilbo is able to quickly conjure from one of his pantries. This flan, a baked pie, uses apples and apricot jelly.*

MAKES FOUR
PREP AND COOK 50 MINUTES, PLUS CHILLING 30 MINUTES

INGREDIENTS

12 ounces ready-made puff pastry sheets
All-purpose flour, for dusting
2 crisp green dessert apples (such as Granny Smith), peeled, cored and sliced
1 tablespoon superfine sugar
2 tablespoons unsalted butter, chilled
Cream or crème fraîche, to serve

For the apricot glaze
1 cup apricot jelly
2 teaspoons lemon juice
2 teaspoons water

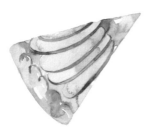

Previous Page:
Bag End

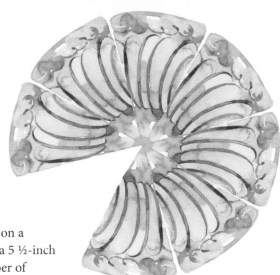

1 Divide the pastry into quarters and roll each out on a lightly floured surface until ⅛-inch thick. Using a 5 ½-inch plate as a guide, cut out 4 rounds—make a number of short cuts around the plate rather than drawing the knife around, which can stretch the pastry. Place the rounds on a baking sheet.

2 Place a slightly smaller plate on each pastry round and score around the edge to form a ½-inch border. Prick the centers with a fork and chill for 30 minutes.

3 Arrange the apple slices in a circle over the pastry rounds and sprinkle with the sugar. Grate the butter over the top and bake in a preheated oven, 425°F, for 25 to 30 minutes until the pastry and apples are golden.

4 Meanwhile, make the apricot glaze. Put the jelly in a small saucepan with the lemon juice and water, and heat gently until the jelly melts. Increase the heat and boil for 1 minute, then remove from the heat and press through a fine sieve. Keep warm, then brush over each apple pie while they are still warm. Serve with cream or crème fraîche.

APPLE AND BLACKBERRY CAKE

Apples and blackberries reach their peak in early fall and what better way to enjoy them than in a cake? Enjoy at teatime or with a cup of coffee after dinner. Store in an airtight tin for up to 2 days.

This crumble cake evokes the fruitfulness of late summer in the Shire—and by extension the Warwickshire of Tolkien's youth—when the trees are laden with apples and the blackberries are bursting with juice. One of Hobbits' chief pastimes is calling on one another—and, to that end, we don't think any Hobbit pantry would have been complete without several nice cakes ready to serve to guests or to enjoy alone while writing thank-you letters to friends for their unwanted birthday gifts.

SERVES SIXTEEN
PREP AND COOK 1 ¼ HOURS

INGREDIENTS

¾ cup butter, at room temperature
1 cup superfine sugar
3 eggs, beaten
1 ½ cups self-rising flour
1 teaspoon baking powder
Grated zest of 1 lemon
3 cups cooking apples, cored, peeled
   and thinly sliced
1 cup frozen blackberries,
   just thawed

For the crumble topping
About ½ cup self-rising flour
¾ cup muesli
¼ cup superfine sugar
6 tablespoons butter, diced

1   Line a 7 x 11-inch roasting pan with nonstick parchment
    paper.

2   Cream the butter and sugar together in a mixing bowl
    until pale and creamy. Gradually mix in alternate
    spoonfuls of beaten egg and flour until all has been added
    and the mixture is smooth. Stir in the baking powder and
    lemon zest, then spoon the mixture into the prepared pan.
    Spread the surface level, then arrange the apple slices and
    blackberries over the top.

3   Make the crumble topping. Put the flour, muesli, and
    superfine sugar in a mixing bowl, add the butter and rub in
    with your fingertips until the mixture resembles fine bread
    crumbs. Sprinkle over the top of the fruit.

4   Bake in a preheated oven, 350°F, for about
    45 minutes until the crumble is golden brown and a
    skewer inserted into the center comes out clean.

5   Leave to cool in the pan, then lift out using the lining
    paper. Cut the cake into 16 bars or wedges and peel off
    the lining paper

BILBO'S ELEVENTY-FIRST BIRTHDAY CAKE

For chocolate lovers, make a chocolate and raspberry version of this cake by replacing ⅕ cup of the flour with ¼ cup of cocoa powder, swapping the strawberries for raspberries, and using raspberry jelly for the filling. For an even more indulgent birthday treat, grate dark chocolate over the cake to finish.

The Lord of the Rings opens with a magnificent feast—a party to celebrate Bilbo Baggins' eleventy-first birthday. Hobbits come from near and far to attend the party, and Gandalf puts on a firework show featuring a dragon in his honor. The big surprise of the night is Bilbo's farewell speech and sudden disappearance as he slips on the One Ring, and secretly leaves Bag End for his last adventure and retirement to Rivendell.

This birthday cake recipe can be made in various versions to please a crowd of even the most demanding Hobbits or humans. Experiment with using different jellies and berries to further customize this cake for your own long-awaited party.

SERVES TWELVE
PREP AND COOK 1 ½ HOURS

INGREDIENTS

¾ cup unsalted butter, softened
¼ teaspoon salt
1 cup superfine sugar
2 teaspoons vanilla extract
2 ¼ cups self-rising flour
2 teaspoons baking powder
3 eggs
About ⅓ cup ground rice
½ cup plain yogurt
1 ¼ cups strawberries, hulled and cut into wedges

To finish
1 cup heavy cream
3 tablespoons strawberry jelly

1   Grease and base line two 8-inch cake
    pans.

2   Put the butter, salt, sugar, and vanilla
    in a food processor and blend until
    smooth. Sift in the flour and baking
    powder, add the eggs, ground rice, and
    yogurt, and whizz together until creamy.

3   Divide the mixture between the
    prepared pans and level the surface.
    Bake in a preheated oven, 350°F,
    for 35 to 40 minutes until risen, golden,
    and springy to the touch.

4   Leave to cool in the pans for 10 minutes,
    then turn out on to a wire rack and
    peel off the lining paper. Leave to
    cool completely.

5   Whip the cream in a bowl until soft
    peaks form. Cut the top off one of
    the cakes to level it, then spread
    with the jelly and then half of the
    cream to the edge. Scatter with two-
    thirds of the strawberries. Place the
    second cake on top and spread with
    the remaining cream.

6   Decorate the top with the remaining
    strawberries. Add candles.

The Day of Bilbo's Party

FOOD AND THE ELVES

Like the Elves themselves, Tolkien typically describes their food and their consumption of it in ethereal terms. While Hobbits, Dwarves, and Men are often shown in the gross act of eating and drinking, feeling hungry, or being greedy, Elves are rarely so depicted. When we do hear about Elvish eating habits, it is generally in vague, somewhat elevated terms. In contrast to the almost food-obsessive *Hobbit* and *The Lord of the Rings*, the Elven-dominated *Silmarillion* is much shorter on references to food, with references to generic feasts rather than to specific foodstuffs or dishes. The overall impression we gain, then, is that for the Elves food is somehow divorced from their bodily needs. They are immortal, after all.

That said, Tolkien's conception of the Elves and their appetites seems to have gone through something of an evolution between the writing of *The Hobbit* and *The Lord of the Rings*. In *The Hobbit*, Bilbo's first encounter with Elves during the Quest of Erebor takes place in Rivendell where, up at the Last Homely House, meatballs are being roasted and bannocks baked—quite earthy foods, to say the least. And in his second encounter, deep in Mirkwood, the starving Bilbo and the Dwarves stumble across a woodland feast at which meats, with enchanting smells, are being roasted over open fires. The Elvenking of Mirkwood, moreover, is depicted as a wine connoisseur, importing fine vintages from as far away as the Sea of Rhûn, and coveting his wine cellar like a Dragon guarding its hoard of gold.

By contrast, our first encounter with Elves in *The Lord of the Rings* provides a very different impression of Elvish appetites, though in part this may be explained by the distinction Tolkien makes between the super-civilized High Elves and the more rustic Wood-elves shown in *The Hobbit*. At Woodhall, Frodo, Pippin, and Sam enjoy a rarefied, seemingly vegetarian meal courtesy of the Noldorin Elf Gildor, featuring bread "surpassing the savor of a fair white loaf" and "fruits sweet as wildberries," washed down by a "fragrant draught, cool as a clear fountain." The foods, it is noticeable, are described in the vaguest terms, as *like* something else—as strange, exotic, and even otherworldly, contrasting strongly with the Hobbits' own robust diet.

Later, much longer encounters with the Elves provide us with even less detail. In Rivendell, there is much feasting, but the primary occupation at such feasts seems almost to be singing and storytelling rather than eating. Similarly, we learn little about food in Lothlórien—except that it is, inevitably, better than the food the Fellowship has been habitually eating. The sole exception is the near-miraculous Lembas Bread (page 54) and the reviving cordial Miruvor (page 163).

DINNER AND SUPPER

Dinner/supper is the most frequently mentioned meal in The Lord of the Rings, *with breakfast a close second—closely reflecting the importance they have in the Hobbits' daily routine. As the heartiest and merriest meal of the day, dinner is much looked forward to and is often accompanied by dinner songs, an example of which is sung by Frodo at the Prancing Pony. The Men of Gondor accord the same importance to supper—which they call the "daymeal"—a time of mirth and relaxation after a hard day's work broken only by a relatively light breakfast and "nuncheon" (noontime lunch).*

HARADRIM TAGINE

This vegetable-filled tagine will prove a winner for meat eaters, vegans, and vegetarians alike. For added nutrition, you could serve it with protein-rich quinoa rather than the traditional couscous, and dried apricots work well in place of the figs.

The Haradrim are a proud, warlike people who live in the dry sunny lands to the south of Gondor. They are ancient enemies of Gondor due to their historic oppression by Númenórean colonizers and fall under the influence of Sauron during the War of the Ring. Tolkien describes them as fond of scarlet and gold, which they use in their jewelry, body paint, armor, and decorations for their war Oliphaunts.

This recipe imagines a Haradrim meal of rich red tomatoes and golden couscous with spices to evoke their bright sunny homeland.

SERVES FOUR
PREP AND COOK 1 HOUR

INGREDIENTS

3 ½ ounces sunflower oil, divided use
1 large onion, finely chopped
2 garlic cloves, crushed
2 teaspoons each ground coriander, cumin, cinnamon
14-ounce can chickpeas, drained
14-ounce can chopped tomatoes
2 cups vegetable stock
¼ teaspoon saffron threads
1 large eggplant, trimmed, and chopped
3 cups button mushrooms, trimmed and halved if large
⅔ cup dried figs, chopped
2 tablespoons chopped fresh cilantro
Salt and black pepper

For the couscous
About 2 cups couscous
½ teaspoon sea salt
1 ¾ cups warm water
1 to 2 tablespoons sunflower oil
2 tablespoons butter, cut into small pieces

1   To make the tagine, heat 2 tablespoons of the oil in a skillet, add the onion, garlic, and spices and cook over medium heat, stirring frequently, for 5 minutes until golden. Using a slotted spoon, transfer to a saucepan and add the chickpeas, tomatoes, stock, and saffron. Season with salt and pepper.

2   Heat the remaining oil in the skillet, add the eggplant, and cook over high heat, stirring frequently, for 5 minutes until browned. Add to the tagine and bring to a boil, then reduce the heat, cover, and simmer gently for 20 minutes.

3   Meanwhile, pour the couscous into an ovenproof dish. Stir the salt into the measured water and pour over the couscous. Stir once to make sure all the grains are submerged in the water, then cover with a clean dishtowel and leave to stand for 10 to 15 minutes.

4   Stir the mushrooms and figs into the tagine and simmer gently, uncovered, for an additional 20 minutes. Stir in the fresh cilantro and adjust the seasoning.

5   Meanwhile, rake a fork through the couscous to break up the grains. Then, using your fingers, rub the oil into the grains until light, airy, and any lumps are broken up. Scatter the butter over and cover with a piece of damp waxed paper. Place in a preheated oven, 350°F, for 15 minutes until heated through.

6   Divide the couscous between 4 plates and spoon over the tagine.

SQUASH AND GOAT CHEESE BAKE

Roasting vitamin-rich beets and squash really brings out their sweet, mellow flavors. Serve this with a pile of peppery, aromatic arugula leaves for a delicious contrast in taste and texture. And, if there's any left over, keep it as a colorful topping for tomorrow's lunchtime salad.

The Shire is meant to be a mythical representation of England rather than a direct copy of some medieval historical reality. Thus, the foods that Tolkien mentions so freely in his tales are inspired primarily by the cooking of his youth, evoking a sense of Englishness that stands outside of time. In this spirit, this recipe combines a vegetable from the New World, squash, with one from the Old World, beets, to create a dish that is both filling and vegetarian-friendly.

SERVES FOUR
PREP AND COOK 50 MINUTES

INGREDIENTS

6 raw beets, peeled and diced
4 ½ cups squash or butternut squash, peeled, deseeded, and cut into slightly larger dice than the beets
1 red onion, cut into wedges
2 tablespoons olive oil
2 teaspoons fennel seeds
2 small goat cheeses, ½ cup each
Salt and black pepper
Chopped rosemary, to garnish

1 Put the vegetables into a roasting pan, drizzle with the oil, and sprinkle with the fennel seeds and salt and pepper. Roast in a preheated oven, 400°F, for 20 to 25 minutes, turning once, until well browned and tender.

2 Cut the goat cheeses into thirds and nestle among the roasted vegetables. Sprinkle the cheeses with a little salt and pepper and drizzle with some of the pan juices.

3 Return the dish to the oven and cook for about 5 minutes until the cheese is just beginning to melt. Sprinkle with rosemary and serve immediately.

THE GREEN DRAGON'S MUSHROOM AND LEEK PIE

These individual pies make a great vegetarian main course. You can also make one large pie, in which case you need to increase the baking time to 20 to 25 minutes or until the pastry is beautifully puffy and golden brown.

Pies don't need to have meat to be warm and comforting. This vegetarian pub classic will make you feel like a Hobbit settling down to a hearty dinner in the Green Dragon in Bywater—Sam and his father's local—gossiping all the while about that odd Mr. Baggins up at Bag End and his fabulous hidden treasure. Whatever—you ask your companion, Andwise Roper—will he do next?

SERVES FOUR
PREP AND COOK 45 MINUTES

INGREDIENTS

2 tablespoons butter
2 leeks, trimmed, cleaned and thinly sliced
3 ¾ cups cremini mushrooms, trimmed and quartered
3 ¾ cups button mushrooms, trimmed and quartered
1 tablespoon all-purpose flour
1 cup milk
½ cup heavy cream
1 cup strong cheddar cheese, grated
¼ cup finely chopped parsley
2 sheets of ready-rolled puff pastry
Beaten egg, to glaze

1 Melt the butter in a large saucepan. Add the leeks and cook over medium heat for 1 to 2 minutes. Add the two kinds of mushrooms and cook for 2 minutes. Stir in the flour for 1 minute, then gradually add the milk and cream, and stir constantly until the sauce boils and thickens. Add the cheddar and parsley, and stir for an addtional 1 to 2 minutes. Remove from the heat.

2 Cut 4 rounds from the pastry sheets to cover 4 individual pie dishes. Divide the mixture between the dishes. Brush the rims with the egg, place the pastry rounds on top, press down slightly and crimp the edges. Cut two slits in the top of each pie to let the steam out. Brush the pastry with the remaining egg.

3 Bake in a preheated oven, 425°F, for 15 to 20 minutes until the pastry is golden. Serve hot.

FELL WINTER ROOT VEGETABLE STEW

This flavorful vegan stew is packed with health-giving vegetables and is perfect for feeding a crowd. The flavor improves on keeping so it tastes even better the next day, gently reheated. Serve with crusty bread or garlic mashed potatoes.

In 2911–12 TA Eriador is struck with a long, cold winter in which food runs short and White Wolves come south, even crossing over the frozen Brandywine river into the Shire. The beleaguered inhabitants of the Shire are only able to survive with the help of Gandalf and the Rangers of the North.

This stew makes use of winter vegetables and dried herbs, conjuring a taste of what we think Hobbits might have eaten during that long cold winter while eagerly awaiting the spring. With each bite, imagine sitting by the hearth as the snow falls down outside, grateful for the warmth and comfort of your well-appointed Hobbit hole.

SERVES EIGHT TO TEN
PREP AND COOK 2 TO 2 ½ HOURS

INGREDIENTS

1 squash or large butternut squash
¼ cup olive oil
1 large onion, finely chopped
4 garlic cloves, finely chopped
1 small red chili, deseeded and chopped
4 celery sticks, cut into 1-inch lengths
4 medium carrots, cut into 1-inch pieces
2 medium parsnips, cut into 1-inch pieces
2 x 14-ounce cans plum tomatoes
3 tablespoons tomato paste
1 to 2 tablespoons hot paprika
1 cup vegetable stock
1 bouquet garni (a bundle of parsley, thyme and bay leaf)
2 x 14-ounce cans red kidney beans, drained and rinsed
Salt and black pepper
¼ cup finely chopped parsley, to garnish

1   Slice the squash or butternut squash in half and discard
    the seeds and fibers. Cut the flesh into cubes, removing the
    skin. You should have about 2 pounds of flesh.

2   Heat the oil in a large saucepan over medium heat, add
    the onion, garlic, and chili and fry until softened but not
    browned. Add the squash or butternut and celery and fry
    gently for 10 minutes.

3   Stir in the carrots, parsnips, tomatoes, tomato paste,
    paprika, stock, and bouquet garni. Bring to a boil, then
    reduce the heat, cover the pan and simmer for 1 to 1 ½
    hours or until the vegetables are almost tender.

4   Add the beans and cook for 10 minutes. Remove and
    discard the bouquet garni. Season with salt and pepper
    and sprinkle with the parsley.

SPINACH AND TOMATO DAHL

Cheap, filling, tasty, and healthy, too, this vegan dahl with its fragrant Indian-spiced oil, is sure to become a regular dinner favorite. Serve with naan bread or steamed basmati rice.

Tolkien tells us that among the Istari, the five Wizards sent to Middle-earth by the Valar in 1000 TA, are the two Blue Wizards—Alatar and Pallando—who travel to regions in the east of Middle-earth, lands—loosely inspired by ancient India, Persia, and China. Tolkien tells us almost nothing of the Blue Wizards' fate, but perhaps they simply fell in love with the cultures of the East, including their richly spiced cuisines.

SERVES FOUR
PREP AND COOK 1 HOUR 10 MINUTES

INGREDIENTS

1 cup dried red split lentils
½ teaspoon ground turmeric
2 green chilies, deseeded and chopped
2 teaspoons peeled and grated ginger
3 ½ cups water
14-ounce can chopped tomatoes
5 cups baby spinach leaves
Salt

For the spiced oil

1 tablespoon sunflower oil
1 shallot, thinly sliced
12 curry leaves
1 teaspoon black mustard seeds
1 teaspoon cumin seeds
1 dried red chili, broken into small pieces

1   To make the dahl, rinse and drain the lentils. Place them in a large saucepan with the turmeric, chilies, ginger, and measured water. Bring to a boil, then reduce the heat and simmer, uncovered, for 40 minutes or until the lentils have broken down and the mixture has thickened.

2   Add the tomatoes and cook for an additional 10 minutes or until thickened. Stir in the spinach and cook for 2 to 3 minutes until wilted.

3   Prepare the spiced oil. Heat the oil in a small skillet, add the shallot, and cook over medium-high heat, stirring, for 2 to 3 minutes until golden brown. Add all the remaining ingredients and cook, stirring constantly, for 1 to 2 minutes until the seeds start to pop.

4   Pour the spiced oil into the dahl, stir well, and season to taste with salt.

TÚRIN TURAMBAR TARRAGON CHICKEN

With its delicate, licorice-like taste, tarragon is the perfect flavor-pairing for chicken. Serve with a green salad, if desired. The chicken can also be served on top of creamy mashed potatoes, instead of pasta.

Tolkien's hero Túrin Turambar lives a life of valiant deeds that culminate in his defeat of the dreaded dragon Glaurung. His tragic story, told in part in The Silmarillion, *finds its fullest rendition in Tolkien's posthumously published* The Children of Húrin, *edited by Christopher Tolkien. We like to think the delicious dish below might well have given this stern, grief-stricken hero a few moments' respite during his hapless struggle to overcome the doom laid on his family by the evil Morgoth.*

SERVES FOUR
PREP AND COOK 20 MINUTES

INGREDIENTS

About 3 cups mostaccioli pasta
Salt
¼ cup olive oil
1 pound skinless chicken breast fillets,
  cut into thin strips
3 medium zucchini, thinly sliced
1 large onion, thinly sliced
2 teaspoons crushed garlic
¼ cup pine nuts
Finely grated zest and juice of 2 lemons
½ cup chopped tarragon
7 ounces crème fraîche
Grated Parmesan cheese, to serve

1 Cook the pasta in a large saucepan of lightly salted boiling water for 8 to 10 minutes or according to the packet instructions

2 Meanwhile, heat the oil in a large skillet, add the chicken, and cook for 3 to 4 minutes until starting to turn golden. Add the zucchini and onion, then cook for an additional 5 minutes until golden and the chicken is cooked through.

3 Add the garlic and pine nuts and cook, stirring, for 2 minutes, then add the lemon zest and juice, tarragon, and crème fraîche, and stir well until hot but not boiling.

4 Drain the pasta, then add to the sauce and toss well to coat. Serve with grated Parmesan.

FISH AND CHIPS

This quintessentially British dish is given a healthy twist as both the French fries and the fish are oven-roasted, rather than deep-fried, and is enhanced by the addition of a creamy dip bursting with citrus flavor for dunking your fries.

We encounter fish and chips in The Lord of the Rings *when Sam reminisces on the good food he could have back home and promises to make the dish for Gollum if he's good. This food might seem anachronistic given the swords and great halls that lend the rest of the book a very medieval feel, but its presence is part and parcel with Tolkien's project of creating a mythology for England. There's nothing more quintessentially English, or indeed British, than fish and chips, and this classic comfort food feels like an element of Britishness that transcends time.*

SERVES FOUR
PREP AND COOK 1 HOUR

INGREDIENTS

9 large floury potatoes, cut into thick
 French fries
2 tablespoons olive oil
About 2 cups whole-wheat bread
 crumbs
Finely grated zest of 1 lemon
3 tablespoons chopped parsley
4 chunky white fish fillets, about 6 ¼ to
 7 ounces each, each cut into 4 chunky
 pieces
About ½ cup all-purpose flour
1 egg, beaten

For the lemony mayonnaise dip
1 egg
½ cup olive oil
1 tablespoon white wine vinegar
Grated zest of 1 small lemon, plus
 2 tablespoons juice
2 tablespoons chopped parsley

1 Toss the potato French fries with the oil,
then roast in a preheated oven, 400°F, for
30 to 40 minutes, turning occasionally until
golden and crisp.

2 Meanwhile, toss the bread crumbs with the
lemon zest and parsley on a plate. Lightly coat
the fish pieces in the flour, then the beaten
egg, and finally the bread crumbs. Place on a
baking sheet and roast alongside the French
fries for the final 20 minutes of the fries'
cooking time until the fish is opaque and
cooked through.

3 For the lemony mayonnaise dip, place the
egg, olive oil, and white wine vinegar in a jug
and whizz with a hand-blender until a thick
mayonnaise is formed. Fold in the lemon zest
and juice, along with the parsley.

BRANDYWINE FISH PIE

A good fish pie is one of the greatest comfort foods. Packed full of flavor, this creamy pie needs nothing more to accompany it than a simple tomato salad or some crunchy steamed green veggies.

Most Hobbits, Tolkien tells us, can't swim. (Long before The Lord of the Rings *begins Frodo's parents have tragically died in a boating accident.) But the author also tells us there is an exception: those Brandybucks across the river in Buckland, who dabble about in boats and are consequently considered a bit odd. The pub in Stock, the Golden Perch, is named after such a fish as the intrepid, weird Brandybucks might have caught from the river nearby.*

SERVES FOUR
PREP AND COOK 1 HOUR 30 MINUTES, PLUS INFUSING

INGREDIENTS

10 ounces peeled and deveined raw shrimp (thawed if frozen)
10 ounces white fish fillets such as haddock, skinned and cut into small pieces
2 teaspoons cornstarch
2 teaspoons green peppercorns in brine, rinsed and drained
1 small fennel bulb, roughly chopped
1 small leek, trimmed, cleaned and roughly chopped
1 ½ cup dill
1 ½ cup Italian parsley
⅔ cup fresh or frozen green peas
5 baking potatoes, thinly sliced
¾ cup cheddar cheese, grated
Salt and black pepper

For the cheese sauce

1 cup, plus 2 tablespoons milk
1 small onion
1 bay leaf
4 tablespoons butter
About ⅓ cup all-purpose flour
1 cup cheddar or Gruyère cheese, grated

Previous Page:
Brandywine River

1   Make the cheese sauce. Put the milk, onion, and bay leaf in a saucepan. Heat until just boiling, then remove from the heat and leave to infuse for 20 minutes. Strain the milk into a jug. Melt the butter in another saucepan, add in the flour and stir in quickly. Cook, stirring, for 1 to 2 minutes, then, off the heat, gradually whisk in the milk mixture until blended. Bring gently to a boil, stirring, and cook for 2 minutes. Off the heat, stir in the grated cheddar or Gruyère.

2   Dry the shrimp, if frozen and thawed, by patting between sheets of paper towel. Pat dry the fish fillets. Season the cornstarch with salt and pepper and use to coat the shrimp and white fish.

3   Lightly crush the peppercorns using a mortar and pestle. Put the peppercorns in a food processor with the fennel, leek, dill, parsley, and a little salt, and blend until very finely chopped, scraping the mixture down from the sides of the bowl if necessary. Ladle into a shallow ovenproof dish.

4   Scatter the shrimp and fish over the fennel mixture, and mix together a little. Scatter the peas on top. Spoon half the cheese sauce over the filling, and spread roughly with the back of a spoon. Layer the potatoes on top, overlapping the slices and seasoning each layer with salt and pepper as you go. Spoon the remaining sauce over the top, spreading it in a thin layer. Sprinkle with the cheese.

5   Bake in a preheated oven, 425°F, for 30 minutes until the surface has turned pale golden. Reduce the oven temperature to 350°F, and cook for an additional 30 to 40 minutes until the potatoes are completely tender and the fish is cooked through.

NÚMENÓREAN RED SNAPPER AND VINE-LEAF PARCELS

A taste of the Mediterranean, this is a meal that will wow guests. The vine leaves will add a lovely astringency to the fish but, if you can't find them, use parchment paper. If you struggle to find red snapper, your local fishmonger or fish counter should be able to advise on a replacement.

In the Second Age, Númenor is a great island-kingdom located in the Sundering Seas, west of Middle-earth, created as a reward for the Men who joined the Elves and the Valar in the struggle against Morgoth. The Númenóreans are granted long lives and became known for their great craftsmanship and prowess as seafarers.

These red snapper and vine leaf parcels are inspired by the calm, warm waters that surround this "isle of the blessed." They are the perfect grilled main for a warm summer's day. Enjoy them with a warm Fig and Prosciutto Salad with blue cheese (page 76) for a Númenórean-inspired feast.

SERVES FOUR
PREP <u>AND</u> COOK 30 MINUTES

INGREDIENTS

¼ cup, plus 2 tablespoons olive oil
2 tablespoons lemon juice
2 tablespoons chopped dill
2 scallions, chopped
1 teaspoon mustard powder
8 vine leaves in brine, drained
4 red snapper, about 12 ounces. each,
   scaled and gutted
4 bay leaves
4 dill sprigs, plus extra to garnish
Salt and black pepper
Lemon wedges, to garnish

1   Put 4 pieces of string, about 12 inches long, into cold water to soak for 10 minutes.

2   Put the oil, lemon juice, chopped dill, scallions, mustard powder, and salt and pepper in a bowl and mix well. Wash and dry the vine leaves and arrange them in pairs, overlapping them slightly.

3   Make several slashes on both sides of each fish and rub them all over with a little of the oil and lemon mixture. Stuff each of the belly cavities with a bay leaf and a dill sprig. Lay each fish on a pair of vine leaves and wrap securely. Brush with a little of the oil and lemon mixture, and fasten with the wet string to secure the leaves in place.

4   Grill the fish on a hot barbecue or under a preheated hot broiler for 4 to 5 minutes on each side, brushing them with a little more of the oil and lemon mixture if necessary, until lightly charred.

5   Leave the fish to rest for a few minutes, then discard the string and vine leaves and dress the snapper with the rest of the oil and lemon mixture. Garnish with dill sprigs.

ROSEMARY LAMB SKEWERS

For a Middle Eastern take on this recipe, make the lamb skewers as below and stuff inside warmed pita breads, along with some shredded lettuce, sliced tomatoes, and a drizzle of sauce made by mixing plain yogurt and tahini with a little lemon juice.

SERVES FOUR
PREP AND COOK 15 MINUTES, PLUS CHILLING

INGREDIENTS

1 pound boneless leg of lamb, minced
1 small onion, finely chopped
1 garlic clove, crushed
1 tablespoon chopped rosemary
6 anchovies in oil, drained and chopped
Olive oil, for brushing
Salt and black pepper

For the tomato and olive salad
6 ripe tomatoes, cut into wedges
1 red onion, sliced
⅔ cup pitted black olives
A few torn basil leaves
Salt and pepper
3 tablespoons extra virgin olive oil
A squeeze of lemon juice

1 Combine the lamb, onion, garlic, rosemary, anchovies, and some salt and pepper in a bowl and use your hands to work them together. Divide into 12 portions and shape into even-sized, sausage-shaped patties. Chill for 30 minutes.

2 Thread the patties on to metal skewers, brush lightly with oil and grill on a hot barbecue or under a preheated hot broiler for 3 to 4 minutes on each side until cooked through.

3 Meanwhile, make the salad. Combine the tomatoes, onion, olives, and basil in a bowl and season with salt and pepper. Drizzle with oil and squeeze a little lemon juice over. Serve the skewers with the salad.

The House of Marach (later known as the House of Hador) is the third kindred of Men (or Edain) to migrate into Beleriand during the First Age. They are the most warlike of the Edain, the most numerous, and the tallest and fairest—most of the great heroes among Men in The Silmarillion *belong to or are descended from this house.*

These grilled lamb skewers are inspired by the House of Marach's long journey into Beleriand out of the east, bringing their sheep, goats, and horses with them. The Men would have cooked over open fires in their campsites, which we approximate with a barbecue. A grill pan on the stovetop will give you similar results.

JUNIPER ROAST LAMB

Mouthwateringly succulent, this roast lamb adds juniper berries to the classic Italian trio of garlic, rosemary, and anchovies for the paste. Make sure you really pound the paste as the smoother it is, the deeper it will penetrate into the meat.

One of the first adventures that Bilbo has after leaving the Shire with Thorin and Company is an encounter with three ill-tempered Trolls, humorously named William, Bert, and Tom. The trolls are "toasting" mutton on a spit and drinking ale, all the while complaining about the monotony of their diet. Perhaps the recipe below might have convinced the Trolls otherwise, and what's more, it needs just a plain old oven, not a tricky-to-handle spit!

SERVES SIX
PREP AND COOK 2 HOURS

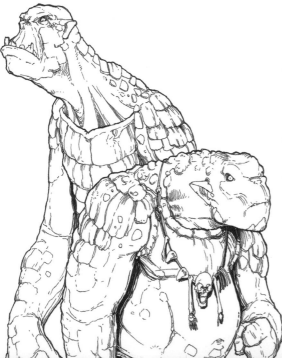

INGREDIENTS

2 tablespoons olive oil
1 leg of lamb, about 3 pounds, trimmed
   of excess fat
10 juniper berries, 6 crushed and 4
   whole reserved
3 garlic cloves, crushed
2 ounces salted anchovies, boned and
   rinsed
1 tablespoon chopped rosemary, plus 2
   rosemary sprigs
2 tablespoons balsamic vinegar
1 cup dry white wine
Salt and black pepper

1 Heat the oil in a roasting pan in which the lamb will fit snugly. Add the lamb and cook until browned all over. Leave to cool.

2 Pound 6 of the juniper berries, the garlic, anchovies, and chopped rosemary with the end of a rolling pin in a bowl. Stir in the vinegar and mix to a paste.

3 Make small incisions all over the lamb with a small, sharp knife. Spread the paste over the lamb, working it into the incisions. Season with salt and pepper.

4 Put the rosemary sprigs in the roasting pan and put the lamb on top. Pour in the wine and add the remaining juniper berries. Cover the roasting pan with foil and bring to a boil, then cook in a preheated oven, 325°F, for 1 hour, turning the lamb every 20 minutes.

5 Increase the temperature to 400°F, uncover and roast for an additional 30 minutes until the lamb is very tender.

6 Serve with the Honey-spiced Carrot and Parsnip Star (page 82) and a helping of roast potatoes.

Trolls

LAKE-TOWN BEEF POT ROAST

This will fill the house with mouthwatering aromas as it cooks and the slow-cooked brisket will be melt-in-the-mouth tender. Serve with some crisp green beans and buttery mashed potatoes or sweet potatoes to mop up the delicious gravy.

SERVES FOUR
PREP AND COOK 2 ½ HOURS

INGREDIENTS

1 ¾ pounds brisket of beef, cut into 2-inch pieces
1 celery stick
2 bay leaves
2 ½ cups full-bodied red wine
1 cup beef or chicken stock
2 carrots, cut at an angle into 1 ½-inch slices
20 baby onions, peeled but kept whole
Salt and black pepper

For the horseradish dumplings
Generous 1 cup self-rising flour
⅓ cup shredded lard
2 teaspoons creamed horseradish
3 tablespoons snipped chives
5 to 7 tablespoons water
Salt and black pepper

1 Season the beef with salt and pepper, and put in a large, flameproof casserole with a tight-fitting lid. Add the celery and bay leaves, then pour in the wine and stock. Bring to a boil, then reduce the heat to a barely visible simmer and cook, covered, for 1 ½ hours, stirring occasionally.

2 Meanwhile, make the dumplings. Mix the flour, lard, horseradish, chives, and salt and pepper in a bowl. Stir in enough water to make a soft but not sticky dough. With floured hands, shape into 8 balls.

3 Add the carrots, onions, and dumplings to the stew. Re-cover and simmer gently for an additional 45 minutes until the dumplings are light and fluffy, adding a little water if the sauce becomes too thick. Remove the beef from the heat and serve.

Lake Town

Bilbo is the Odysseus of Tolkien's world, his heroism defined not so much by his bravery or skill in arms, but by his cunning, even duplicity. One of Bilbo's greatest feats of cunning in The Hobbit *occurs when he helps the Dwarves escape their imprisonment by the Elves of Mirkwood by hiding them in the Elvenking's empty wine barrels.*

These wine barrels get sent up and down the river from Mirkwood to Lake-town, where the Men of Lake-town refill them with wine and mead to sell back to the Elves. As the Elves obliviously push the Dwarf-carrying barrels down into the river, they sing them on their way, out into the open pasturelands where the Lake-men's cattle feed. Here we have a smuggling operation as wily as Odysseus' Trojan Horse!

This recipe is inspired by Lake-town's exports to Mirkwood and combines both beef and wine in a slow-cooked roast. Prepare this dish to warm up after a crisp, cold day. It is perfect for feeding a crowd or creating leftovers to eat during the week.

SAM'S CONEY STEW

Rabbit can be a bit dry if not cooked the right way, but braising it slowly in a richly flavored sauce will guarantee tender, juicy meat. Chicken thighs would work well here as a substitute for rabbit.

Samwise's campfire rabbit stew provides one of the most iconic moments in The Lord of the Rings, *providing a scene of comfort and a whiff of home for Frodo and Sam before the final stage of their journey across the mountains into Mordor. Sam bewails the lack of a good stock and "taters," but he does manage to gather up a few herbs to add some flavor. Fortunately, here in the real world we have more ingredients at our disposal than poor Sam has in Ithilien.*

In honor of Master Samwise's stew we have devised this rich and comforting stew that calls upon the flavors of herbs to complement the rich and tender rabbit meat.

SERVES FOUR
PREP AND COOK 2 ¾ HOURS

INGREDIENTS

½ teaspoon ground black pepper
½ teaspoon ground allspice
2 teaspoons finely chopped thyme or
   sage leaves
3 tablespoons olive oil
1 ½ pounds rabbit pieces or skinless
   chicken thighs
3 large onions, sliced
2 teaspoons superfine sugar
3 garlic cloves, crushed
3 ounces red wine vinegar
1 cup red wine
¼ cup tomato paste
Salt
2 bay leaves
Italian parsley, to garnish

1   Mix together the pepper, allspice, and rosemary and rub
    over the rabbit or chicken pieces.

2   Heat the oil in a large, flameproof casserole and fry the
    meat in batches on all sides until thoroughly browned.
    Trasfer the meat to a plate.

3   Add the onions to the pan with the sugar and fry,
    stirring frequently, for about 15 minutes until
    caramelized. Stir in the garlic and cook for an
    additional minute.

4   Add the vinegar and wine to the pan. Bring to
    a boil and continue to boil until the mixture
    has reduced by about a third. Stir in the
    tomato paste and a little salt, return the meat
    to the pan and add the bay leaves.

5   Cover with a lid and place in a preheated oven,
    300°F, for about 2 hours for rabbit and 1½ hours
    if using chicken thighs, until the meat is very
    tender and the juices thick and glossy. Check
    the seasoning and sprinkle with the parsley.

FEASTING IN TOLKIEN

It is no coincidence that both *The Hobbit* and *The Lord of the Rings* begin with feasts, albeit of two somewhat different kinds—an informal, impromptu one in *The Hobbit* when the impeccably hospitable but increasingly flustered Bilbo finds himself forced to cater for a growing number of ravenous Dwarves; and the grand, highly organized one of *The Lord of the Rings*, for which an enormous open-air kitchen is set up and cooks employed from all the inns in the neighborhood—mass-catering on an Oliphaunt-ine scale!

Both of these feasts, different as they are, serve the same basic narrative function. Each conjures up a world of cheerful plenty, with associated feelings of warmth and security, peace and happiness—all the ingredients, in short, that we associate with the word "home." This is the safe place that the comfort-loving Hobbits of both books must leave behind as they set out on their quests into the perilous outside world and begin their transformation into heroes.

Importantly, too, feasting fosters a sense of community: the wily Gandalf knows that the best way to get Bilbo and the Dwarves together is to trick them into eating and drinking together—even if Bilbo is a somewhat unwilling host in his own cozy version of a feasting hall, Bag End!

In *The Two Towers* we encounter an actual feasting hall where Tolkien underlines the Golden Hall's societal function by having Legolas describe it as a light shining over the land. Ironically, when Gandalf, Aragorn, Legolas, and Gimli first come to Meduseld, they find it gloomy and unfriendly, the very antithesis of festive and hospitable. The absence of feasting here symbolizes the rot that has set in at the heart of the kingdom and in the heart of the prematurely aged king, Théoden.

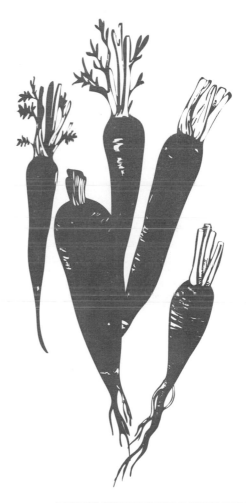

Think of Middle-earth and drinking, and inevitably flowing tankards of ale come to mind, probably enjoyed in one of the many hospitable inns of the Shire or Bree-land. But the many peoples of Tolkien's world consume a much wider range of beverages—both alcoholic and nonalcoholic—from the refreshing Ent-draughts of Fangorn to the hot spiced wines loved by the Dwarves.

AND TO DRINK...

ATHELAS TEA

With its heady scent of mint and lemon verbena, this clean-tasting tea is refreshing and reviving. It's a good aid to digestion after dinner, as an alternative to coffee.

SERVES FOUR
PREP AND COOK 20 MINUTES

INGREDIENTS

2 teaspoons Chinese gunpowder green tea leaves
2 to 3 sugar lumps, plus extra to taste
Large bunch of peppermint and garden mint leaves and stems
Small bunch of lemon verbena leaves and stems

1   Place the green tea and sugar lumps in a teapot. Pour a little boiling water over and leave to steep for 5 minutes.

2   Add the mint and lemon verbena leaves to the pot, packing them in as tightly as you can. Add more sugar to taste and top up the pot with boiling water.

3   Place the teapot over a pan of boiling water or over low heat on the stove, or simply cover with a tea cozy. Leave to brew for 10 minutes.

4   Place 4 tea glasses on a tray. Pour some of the tea into a glass, then pour it back into the pot. Hold the pot high above the glasses and pour slowly so that bubbles form on top of the tea. Serve immediately.

Tolkien imagined his Middle-earth in almost every aspect and in astonishing detail—right down to the smallest herb. Athelas, or Kingsfoil, is a long-stemmed leaf that is used by Aragorn to help heal Frodo after he is wounded by a Nazgûl blade on Weathertop. The plant has a clear, clean, and revitalizing scent that strengthens both body and mind.

Here the flavor of Athelas is imagined as a combination of mint and lemon verbena, offering both comforting warmth and refreshment.

MIRUVOR

Fragrant rose water is the key to this refreshing cordial. Serve it on a hot summer day over lots of ice cubes and with a sprig of mint or slice of cucumber. A dash added to a gin and tonic transforms it into a cocktail full of Eastern promise.

Miruvor is an Elvish reviving cordial made from Yavanna's flowers and used in Elvish festivals. In The Lord of the Rings, *Elrond gifts Gandalf a flask of Miruvor. It comes in handy for the Fellowship when they drink it to revive themselves after braving the treacherous snowy mountain crossing of Caradhras.*

This fragrant drink will warm you up in a pinch and prepare you to overcome the next challenge on your journey—even if it's an abandoned mine hiding a Balrog.

SERVES SIX TO EIGHT
PREP AND COOK 15 MINUTES

INGREDIENTS

2 ¼ cups granulated sugar
7 ½ ounces water
Juice of ½ lemon
3 ½ ounces rose water

1   Place the sugar and measured water in a heavy-bottomed saucepan and bring to a boil, stirring continuously until the sugar has dissolved.

2   Add the lemon juice and simmer for 5 minutes. Stir in the rose water and simmer for 4 to 5 minutes. Leave to cool in the pan, then pass through a sieve into a sterilized bottle or jar.

3   To serve, put a few ice cubes into a glass, add 2 to 3 tablespoons of the cordial, and top up with cold water. The cordial can also be stored in the refrigerator for 3 to 4 weeks.

THE OLD TOOK'S HOT CHOCOLATE

A decadently grown-up take on hot chocolate, this chili-spiked toddy is the perfect antidote to a cold and grey winter day. The chili can be omitted, if you prefer, but it brings a welcome hint of extra heat to the chocolate and rum combination.

The Old Took—properly named Gerontius Took—is the 23rd Thain of the Shire and a venerable ancestor of both Pippin and Merry. We can imagine him, in his very ripe old age, tucked up in a cozy armchair in the Great Smials—the ancestral seat of the Tooks in Tuckborough—sipping this warming hot chocolate with its kick of chili and alcohol. (We should note that, perhaps surprisingly, Tolkien never mentions chocolate in his stories, perhaps because of its New World origins.)

SERVES FOUR
PREP AND COOK 25 MINUTES

INGREDIENTS

About ½ cup cocoa powder
4 teaspoons instant coffee granules
3 ½ cups boiling water, divided use
4 ounces dark rum
½ cup, plus 1 tablespoon superfine sugar
½ teaspoon ground cinnamon
1 large dried or fresh red chili, halved

1 Put the cocoa and instant coffee in a bowl and mix into a smooth paste with half a cup of the boiling water.

2 Pour the cocoa paste into a large saucepan. Add the remaining boiling water, the rum, sugar, cinnamon, and red chili and mix together. Simmer for at least 20 minutes until piping hot.

3 Stir well, then ladle into heatproof glasses.

NONALCOHOLIC VARIATION

SERVES FOUR
PREP <u>AND</u> COOK 10 MINUTES

INGREDIENTS

1 ¾ cups water
4 cardamom pods
3 teaspoons very finely ground Arabica coffee
1 teaspoon cocoa powder
4 teaspoons granulated sugar

1 Place the water and cardamom pods in a small saucepan and carefully spoon the coffee, cocoa powder, and sugar on top. Gently stir the mixture into the surface of the water, making sure you don't touch the bottom of the pan with the spoon.

2 Bring to just below boiling point over medium heat, gradually drawing the outer edges of the mixture into the middle to create a froth. Just as it is about to bubble, spoon some of the froth into 4 coffee cups and pour in the chocolatey coffee. Leave to stand for a minute before drinking to let the coffee grains settle at the bottom of the cups.

Following Page: Orcs

ORC-DRAUGHT

This honey-laced classic winter warmer really packs a punch, and it's a great choice for when you are entertaining.

Orc-draught is a burning yet revitalizing drink that the super-breed of Orcs known as the Uruk-hai force on Merry and Pippin while taking them to Saruman at Isengard. Our reimagining of this drink will numb pain and keep you marching under the banners of darkness for as long as it takes.

SERVES SIX
PREP AND COOK 25 MINUTES

INGREDIENTS

1 ½ cups dry cider
½ cup whiskey
½ cup orange juice
¼ cup honey
2 cinnamon sticks
Orange wedges and curls,
   to decorate (optional)

1 Add all the ingredients to a large saucepan,
   cover with the lid and simmer for 20 minutes
   until piping hot.

2 Stir, then ladle into heatproof glasses. Add
   orange wedges and curls to decorate, if
   desired.

THE MULLED WINES OF MORIA

The delicious smells of spices, fruit, and wine will fill the air when you make these decadent mulled drinks. For something a little different from the usual red mulled wine, try the white wine variation. These drinks are perfect for celebrations on a cold winter day.

RED MULLED WINE

Warming and cheering, with an extra kick from some added brandy.

SERVES SIX
PREP AND COOK 25 MINUTES

INGREDIENTS

1 bottle inexpensive red wine
1 cup clear apple juice
1 cup water
Juice of 1 orange
1 orange, sliced
½ lemon, sliced
1 cinnamon stick, halved
6 cloves
2 bay leaves
⅔ cup superfine sugar
2 ½ cups brandy

1 Pour the wine, apple juice, water, and orange juice into a large saucepan.

2 Add the sliced orange and lemon, the cinnamon stick, cloves, and bay leaves, then mix in the sugar and brandy.

3 Cover with the lid and simmer for at least 20 minutes until piping hot. The longer it simmers the more the flavors will develop. Ladle into heatproof glasses.

WHITE MULLED WINE

Spiced with "Rhûnic" (Eastern) flavors of cardamom, ginger, and star anise this is lighter-bodied and fresher than red mulled wine.

SERVES SIX
PREP AND COOK 15 MINUTES, PLUS STANDING 20 MINUTES

INGREDIENTS

3 ¼ cups white wine
1 cup water
1-inch piece ginger, peeled and thinly sliced
2 star anise
1 cinnamon stick
3 cardamom pods, bruised
2 tablespoons honey
4 cloves
2 strips orange peel, studded with 4 cloves

1 Add the white wine and measured water to a large saucepan. Then add all the remaining ingredients and heat slowly over medium heat until just simmering.

2 Remove from the heat and allow to stand for 20 minutes to mull.

3 To serve, gently reheat the mulled wine and serve warm.

Caves, even beautifully carved and decorated ones, can be rather cold. Of course, the Dwarves of a kingdom like Moria (Khazad-dûm) would have made their cavernous realm comfortable with warm hearths, but still a warm, hearty drink would hardly go amiss after braving the blizzards of the Misty Mountains to reach one of its gates. Here we have two recipes that can be used to liven up even an average bottle of wine imported from the lands of Men.

MEAD

Mead is enjoying a revival among artisan brewers and bartenders in the know. Either make your own, or find it at speciality shops and online and enjoy it the contemporary way with the cocktails opposite.

Mead, also known as honey wine, is one of the oldest fermented beverages in the world, found throughout Europe, Asia, and Africa. You'll also find it everywhere in Middle-earth: Beorn serves mead to Thorin's company in The Hobbit; *Frodo, Sam, and Pippin meet a company of High Elves while still in the Shire in* The Lord of the Rings *and drink a honeyed beverage that sounds very much like mead; and when Celeborn and Galadriel bid farewell to the Fellowship of the Ring they share a drink of white mead to mark the occasion.*

MAKES APPROX. 1.3 GALLONS

PREP 2 HOURS, PLUS 1 YEAR MATURING

INGREDIENTS

1.1 gallons water
3 ¼ cups honey
Juice of 1 lemon
1 vitamin C tablet
1 teaspoon wine yeast

1   Put the water, honey, lemon juice and vitamin C tablet in a large, heavy-based saucepan and bring to a boil to kill the natural yeasts. (You can sterilize the mixture with the appropriate number of proprietary sterilizing tablets if you prefer.)

2   Leave the liquid to cool, then transfer it to a sterilized demijohn. Add the wine yeast and close with a sterilized airlock. The fermentation will take place for around 2 weeks and then the lees will start to settle.

3   Rack (siphon) off the liquid into another sterilized demijohn and store in a cool, dark place. (If you can manage to store it on a heavy stone floor, the sediment will fall more easily.) Siphon off the mead again.

4   When the liquid is clear, transfer it to bottles and store for at least a year—if you can manage to resist it!

MEAD MULE

Fiery ginger ale, sweet mead, and fresh lime combine in this twist on the classic Moscow Mule.

SERVES ONE
PREP 5 MINUTES

INGREDIENTS

2 ounces mead
2 teaspoons lime juice
½ cup ginger ale
Ice cubes

To decorate
Sprig of mint
Lime wedge

1 Add the mead, lime juice, and ginger ale to a mixing glass and stir.

2 Pour into a tumbler over ice cubes and top with the mint sprig and lime wedge.

MEAD FIZZ

Perfect for a celebratory brunch, this recipe adds a dash of mead to enhance the more traditional Buck's Fizz.

SERVES ONE
PREP 5 MINUTES

INGREDIENTS

¼ cup freshly squeezed orange juice
2 tablespoons mead
3 ½ ounces chilled Champagne

1 Add the orange juice and mead to a Champagne flute, mix briefly, then slowly top up with the Champagne.

DRINKS IN MIDDLE-EARTH

There is quite a drinking culture in Middle-Earth, with each of its peoples most closely associated with a particular kind of beverage, usually of the alcoholic kind.

It will come as no surprise that Hobbits—whose culture broadly reflects that of late Victorian and Edwardian England—have a great liking for beer. The Shire has a large number of inns, and beer flows freely at every meal, feast, and celebration. The very best beer in the Eastfarthing, so Pippin claims, is brewed at The Golden Perch in Stock, but the Prancing Pony out at Bree, frequented by both Hobbits and Men, also has an excellent reputation. In the early Fourth Age, an especially good beer would be routinely compared to the superlative beers of 1420 in the Shire Reckoning—the year after the end of the War of the Ring when the Northfarthing barley crop (among many other crops) was so fine.

Men, too, are partial to beer, but mead—made by fermenting honey with water—also seems to be widely drunk, especially by the nobler Mannish peoples, such as the Beornings and Rohirrim, for whose cultures Tolkien took inspiration from the mead-drinking Anglo-Saxons. In *The Hobbit*, Gandalf drinks at least a quart of mead while breakfasting under the roof of Beorn, the Beornings' chieftain, and this sweet, golden beverage must also have been served at the Meduseld, the Golden Hall of the Kings of Rohan, whose very name is derived from the Old English word *maeduselde*, or "mead hall."

While we know there are vineyards in the Southfarthing of the Shire (among Hobbits, Old Winyards is an esteemed *appellation*), wine is most closely associated with the Elves. In *The Hobbit* the Elvenking of Mirkwood is very fond of wine and keeps a prodigiously well-stocked cellar as well as a butler to look after it: his favorite wine is a strong, heady vintage from Dorwinion on the shores of the Sea of Rhûn, hundreds of miles away. We might well imagine that the ultra-civilized Númenóreans and the Gondorians after them are also inveterate wine drinkers.

Not every drink in Middle-earth is alcoholic. The Ents—the guardians of the trees—rather than eating in any conventional sense, take sustenance and refreshment from Ent-draughts, which are made from river water and kept in large stone jars. The draughts seem to have an almost supernatural power to promote growth—Pippin and Merry grow two or three inches taller after consuming Ent-draughts during their time in Fangorn Forest. The Elves, too, have Miruvor, a sustaining herbal cordial (page 163).

INDEX

PICTURE ACKNOWLEDGMENTS

Front cover illustrations:

Dreamstime/Marina Korchagina; iStock/Vikeriya; iStock/Val_Iva; shutterstock/Irina Oksenoyd; shutterstock/curiosity; 123rf/Natalia Hubbert; istock/NataliaHubbert

Back cover illustrations:

Dreamstime/Daria Ustiugova; Dreamstime/Kamenuka; 123RF/Oleksandra Pinchuk

Interiors:

Tim Clarey p.10, p.160; Michael Foreman p.50, p.132; Melvyn Grant p.7, p.74; Pauline Martin p. 101; Mauro Mazzara pp.28–29, p.54, p.63, p.90, p.152, p.155; pp.166–167; Ana Zaja Petrak p.3, p.17, p.36, p.66–67, p.89, p.106, p.151, p.157; Andrea Piparo pp.22–23, pp.40–41, pp.86–87, pp.122–123; Sue Porter p.94; Lidia Postma p.5, p.8, p.58, p.111, pp.118–119, pp.144–145; Sarka Skorpikova p.32, p.104; p.129;

iStock:
Daria Ustiugova p.12–13, p.14, p.42, p.47, p.98, p.113, p.135, p.165, p.171; izumikobayashi pp.124–125; macrovector p.93; Mona Monash p.148; Nata_Kit pp. 127; Natalia Hubbert pp.27; Olya Kamieshkova p.71, p. 83, p.97; Pleshko74 p.57, p.108, p.109, p.115, p.150; Vasabii p.49;

Dreamstime: Marina Korchagina p.78, p.79;

Shutterstock: Arxichtu4ki p.79; Irina Oksenoyd p.70, p.73;

123RF: Natalia Hubbert p.142, p.153; Monamonash pp.18–19, p.25, p.31, pp.38–39, p.46, p.65, p.80, p.81, p.139, p.147, p.168, p.169